Enneagram

A Complete Guide to Finding Your Strengths

(Finding Your Enneagram Type Made Easy)

Oscar Gerhard

Published by Knowledge Icons

Oscar Gerhard

*Enneagram: A Complete Guide to Finding Your Strengths
(Finding Your Enneagram Type Made Easy)*

ISBN 978-1-990084-56-0

Legal & Disclaimer

The information contained in this book is not designed to replace or take the place of any form of medicine or professional medical advice. The information in this book has been provided for educational and entertainment purposes only.

The information contained in this book has been compiled from sources deemed reliable, and it is accurate to the best of the Author's knowledge; however, the Author cannot guarantee its accuracy and validity and cannot be held liable for any errors or omissions. Changes are periodically made to this book. You must consult your doctor or get professional medical advice before using any of the suggested remedies, techniques, or information in this book.

Table of Contents

Introduction

The enneagram (pronounced "any-a-gram") is a system of nine archetypal personality types (or enneatypes) that is based upon an ancient nine-sided symbol (pictured). The word is derived from the Greek words "ennea" (meaning nine) and "gramma" (meaning written or drawn). This unique introduction to the enneagram describes the underlying factors that distinguish the nine enneatypes.

Combining traditional wisdom with modern psychology, the enneagram is a comprehensive, powerful and versatile system for understanding yourself and others. It has a variety of uses, including:

☐Personal development and spiritual growth

☐Developing successful relationships at home and at work

☐Increasing self-awareness and emotional intelligence

☐Increasing personal and professional effectiveness

☐Understanding our patterns of thinking, feeling, and behaving

☐Supporting our strengths and developing our potential

☐Identifying our limitations and associated blind spots

☐Becoming more understanding of other people's behaviors

☐Managing our personal reactivity

Have you ever wondered why you say, think, and do the things you do? If so, why not find out more about Enneagram? You will find this personality typing system fascinating and you will discover the answers to those unanswered questions.

The Enneagram is made up of nine points on a circle, each represented by a number from one to nine. The numbers are used to keep things neutral, and a larger digit does not mean a superior personality type. The nine points represent the nine basic personality types of course, and each type is connected to two others through interconnecting lines.

The lines show very clearly the points a person will head towards when feeling good or under stress. In most cases, there will be arrows on the lines indicating the direction towards the integration or growth points, which means the particular personality type we would move toward when we are feeling good or empowered.

Moving in the opposite direction would indicate the particular personality type we would move toward when under stress. This is known as our disintegration or stress points. Moving toward these points does not mean that we will adopt a new personality altogether but simply that we will exhibit certain characteristics of that particular personality type. When feeling good, we will show some healthy qualities of our growth point. Conversely, we will also show negative traits of our stress points when under pressure.

The Enneagram has been around for many centuries in various forms.

The one I refer to in this article is most commonly referred to as the Enneagram of Personalities, and is a combination of ancient wisdom and modern psychology. The word Enneagram means "9-pointed star" and refers to the traditional depiction of the Enneagram in a diagrammatic form.

The 9 points each refer to a way of viewing the world we live in: how we relate to it and the way it relates to us. The nine ways of viewing the world are the strategies that each one of us has for reacting to situations in which we are either under stress or relaxed. In life, we tend to a adopt one of these strategies in preference to all the others and this has repercussions on how we behave in different circumstances.

A useful analogy in explaining what the Enneagram is, and what it does, is the comparison of humans to computers. A computer has hardware, software, and memory and at its heart there is the operating system, without which the computer cannot operate.

Operating System: Windows XP / Windows Vista / MAC / Linux / other

Hardware: The housing of the computer, CD drive, Hard Drive, etc.

Software: The programs

CPU: The central processing unit, that carries out all the computations in a computer

Memory: The RAM memory

The software allows the computer to carry out specific tasks and the memory (the RAM) along with the central processing unit decides how quickly it can do this.

We are used to upgrading a computer's operating system every few years to benefit from the latest developments in computer technology. So, many of us are using the latest version of Windows by now. We know that if we try to use the latest software with an old operating system, the software will either not work in the way it was designed or not work at all. We also know that the more programs we try to run simultaneously, the more memory we will use up and that the computer will get slower and sometimes it may even crash.

In the human body, we also have a similar setup:

Operating system: One of the nine Enneagram patterns

Hardware: Our body

Software: The skills we have learned in life

Memory: The brain

However, unlike the computer, most of us have never upgraded our operating system to benefit from all of the latest developments (our

life's learning process); in fact, most of us have no idea which operating system we have installed in the first place!

Running an operating system which was first fully installed by the age of two in most cases, and certainly no later than the age of five, we try to use the latest software on it and then we wonder why those skills don't give the result they were supposed to (new software applied to an old operating system). Additionally, we carry around a whole range of unresolved life issues (open program files) which use up larger and larger amounts of our CPU and memory, so we get slower as life goes on and some of us even crash (nervous breakdowns).

This is a very simplified analogy with the computer, but it does explain quiet well the role of the Enneagram patterns in our lives. Just as a computer, we cannot do much without our operating system. And just as with a computer, this operating system limits what we can do according to the rules/limits of that same operating system.

The Enneagram is the way out of this circle of limitation. It gives us knowledge of the primary operating system that governs our every action and then allows us to upgrade that system, so that we begin to operate at full potential. How are we to solve the problems in our lives if we don't know what is causing them in the first place?

The Enneagram model has been found to be very powerful, not only in mapping human behavior, but also in sustainable personal development and transformation processes. It has been used throughout history to enable humans to transcend the self-imposed limitations of their 'operating system'.

The Enneagram is a personality typing system based around nine distinct personality types - the theory being that everyone falls into one of these nine categories. Some say that it is an ancient system with its origins traceable to Sufism, while others suggest that it is much more recent. However, it is an interesting system with more complexity than meets the eye at first glance.

Our personality develops in childhood - it is our coping strategy which we develop in order to be able to deal with our own personal environment. There are nine distinctive patterns recognized in the Enneagram, but the system also predicts how each of the nine personalities will change under stress or when feeling completely secure.

So, why would we want to classify anyone as a specific personality type? Well, despite the fact that we can go to the moon, most of us have huge difficulty understanding each other. A key to being able to understand other people is to first develop a proper understanding of ourselves and one way of doing that is to take a look at yourself via the Enneagram.

It is not an easy thing to put your own personality under the microscope. You have to be prepared to hear and discover things about yourself that you may not necessarily want to know. You may not like some of the things you discover. There is no point in finding out something about yourself if you are not prepared to address the findings. Changing your behavior takes time, work, and a good deal of commitment.

A couple of points to bear in mind when using Enneagram: firstly, we need to recognize that all personality types are essentially positive and that any negative behavior you may become aware of can be remedied; secondly, you should be very careful about "typing" someone else i.e. putting somebody into a specific Enneagram category.

Knowing where someone else sits on the 9 points can certainly lead to an improved understanding of them and better communication. However, the downside is that it can also lead to stereotyping people and that might lead you to associate specific negative reactions with certain people. For example, we run the risk of deciding that because somebody is a type 7, this means that they are uncommitted and always will be. Or if someone is a type 9, they will be lazy. By stereotyping people and trying to predict their reactions, we are imposing our own prejudiced ideas and that's just not a good thing.

As we will see, each of the 9 types of personality has both positive and negative characteristics. This makes perfect sense, since no human being is perfect, but it is not healthy to concentrate on the negative aspects of anyone's character. Accepting people for who they are and not what we want them to be leads to improved communication and more enjoyable human relationships.

The Story of the Locksmith: A Sufi Tale

Once there lived a metalworker, a locksmith, who was unjustly accused of crimes and was sentenced to a deep, dark prison. After he had been there for a while, his wife who loved him very much went to the King and beseeched him that she might at least give him a prayer rug so he could observe his five prostrations every day. The King considered that a lawful request, so he let the woman bring her husband a prayer rug. The prisoner was thankful to get the rug from his wife and every day he faithfully did his prostrations on it.

Much later, the man escaped from prison. When people asked him how he got out, he explained that after years of doing his prostrations and praying for deliverance from prison, he began to see what was right in front of his nose. One day, he suddenly saw that his wife had woven into the prayer rug the pattern of the lock that imprisoned him. Once he realized this and understood that all the information he needed to escape was already in his possession, he began to befriend his guards. He also persuaded the guards that they all would have a better life if they cooperated and escaped the prison together. They agreed since, although they were guards, they realized that they were in prison, too. They also wished to escape, but they had no means to do so.

So the locksmith and his guards decided on the following plan: the guards would bring the locksmith pieces of metal and he would fashion useful items from them to sell in the marketplace. Together they would amass resources for their escape and from the strongest piece of metal they could acquire, the locksmith would fashion a key.

One night, when everything had been prepared, the locksmith and his guards unlocked the prison and walked out into the cool night where his beloved wife was waiting for him. He left the prayer rug behind so that any other prisoner who was clever enough to read the pattern of the rug could also make his escape. Thus, the locksmith was reunited with his loving wife, his former guards became his friends, and everyone lived in harmony. Love and skillfulness prevailed.

This traditional Sufi teaching story, from Idries Shah, can symbolize our study of the Enneagram: the lock is our personality, the prayer rug is the Enneagram, and the key is the Work. Note that although the wife brings the rug, in order to get the tools, the locksmith has to create something useful for his guards. He cannot get out alone or for free. Furthermore, during the whole time, he was praying for deliverance, the means of his liberation was literally "right under his nose," although he never saw the pattern or understood its meaning. One day, however, he woke up, saw it, and then had the means to escape.

The moral of the story is clear: every one of us is in prison. We only have to awaken to "read" the pattern of the lock that will allow us to escape.

Chapter 1: What Is The Enneagram?

The Enneagram is an arrangement of character composing that depicts designs in how individuals conceptualize the world and deal with their feelings. The Enneagram model depicts nine distinctive character types and maps every one of these sorts on a nine-guided graph which helps toward delineate how the sorts identify with each other. The name Enneagram originates from the Greek: Ennea,

the Greek word for nine and Gramma implies something that is drawn or composed.

As indicated by the Enneagram, each character has a specific world view and takes a gander at the world through their very own focal point or channel. This makes it conceivable to clarify why individuals act in specific manners. By portraying how the fundamental character adjusts and reacts to both upsetting and steady circumstances, the Enneagram shows open doors for self-awareness and gives an establishment to the comprehension of others.

The framework has been the motivation for various Enneagram character tests just as books on a diverse assortment of subjects, from self-awareness and otherworldly development, to connections and even profession improvement.

Understanding the Enneagram Symbol

The premise of the Enneagram is a nine-pointed geometric image. It comprises of an external hover, on which the nine (characters) are numbered clockwise and equally separated. There is likewise a triangle between the focuses 9, 3 and 6 and an unpredictable hexagon which interfaces different focuses. The circle speaks to the completeness and solidarity of human life while different shapes speak to how it is isolated.

The sorts on either side of each center kind are called wings. The Enneagram doesn't make any abrupt bounces between the nine sorts, and scarcely any individuals are totally and only a solitary kind. One or both the wings may impact our perspectives and acting and are coordinated into somebody's general character.

Every fundamental sort in the Enneagram is likewise associated by two lines to two other essential sorts; for instance, Type 1 is associated with Type 7 and Type 4. The primary line associates with the sort which the individual has abandoned or quelled in youth; the qualities of this sort must be reintegrated all together for the individual to create. The subsequent line associates with the sort which the individual may develop into once they are prepared to arrive at a higher condition of improvement.

These associating lines feature how every essential sort has fundamental qualities, and yet has darker sides that are loaded with difficulties. The consideration of these lines moves the Enneagram from an absolutely elucidating character model to one that is dynamic, indicating how character can change under various conditions.

History of the Enneagram

We don't have the foggiest idea about the precise root of the Enneagram, yet we do realize it has a varied history. Some accept old roots in Babylon around 4,500 years prior while others place the source in old style Greek way of thinking around 2,500 years back. The model has been credited to the Jewish Kabbalah, Christian otherworldliness and Sufism, a magical type of Islam. Dante evidently had generally excellent information on the Enneagram since the characters in The Divine Comedy relate to a great extent to the Enneagram types.

The reason of the Enneagram is a nine-pointed geometric picture. It contains an outside drift, on which the nine (characters) are numbered clockwise and similarly isolated. There is moreover a triangle between the centers 9, 3 and 6 and an erratic hexagon which interfaces distinctive core interests. The hover addresses the fulfillment and solidarity of human life while various shapes address how it is disengaged.

The sorts on either side of each middle kind are called wings. The Enneagram doesn't make any sudden ricochets between the nine sorts, and barely any people are absolutely and just a single kind. One or both the wings may affect our points of view and acting and are composed into someone's general character.

Each basic sort in the Enneagram is in like manner related by two lines to two other basic sorts; for example, Type 1 is related with Type 7 and Type 4. The essential line partners with the sort which the individual has deserted or suppressed in youth; the characteristics of this sort must be reintegrated all together for the person to make. The consequent line partners with the sort which the individual may form into once they are set up to land at a higher state of progress.

These partner lines highlight how every basic sort has key characteristics, but then has darker sides that are stacked with troubles. The thought of these lines moves the Enneagram from a completely explaining character model to one that is dynamic, showing how a character can change under different conditions.

We don't have the foggiest thought regarding the exact foundation of the Enneagram, yet we do acknowledge it has a shifted history. Some acknowledge old roots in Babylon around 4,500 years earlier while others place the source in old style Greek perspective around 2,500 years back. The model has been credited to the Jewish Kabbalah, Christian supernatural quality and Sufism, an enchanted sort of Islam. Dante clearly had commonly amazing data on the Enneagram since the characters in The Divine Comedy identify with an incredible degree to the Enneagram types.

Chapter 2: The Right One

Congratulations you have reached Section 50.

You are nearly at the end of the Adventure!

Read the following list of personality traits and note which ones you agree with about your own character.

SUMMARY:

*Conscientious and ethical with a strong sense of right and wrong.

*I am often focused on improving myself and I am wary of making mistakes.

*Orderly and fastidious.

*Highly Principled.

*Discerning and wise, realistic and noble.

*Morally Heroic.

*I have a dislike of corruption and I hate injustice.

*I have a desire to be good, to have integrity and to be balanced.

*I am sometimes known as an Idealist or good Advocate

*I feel motivated to improve everything and to be beyond criticism.

DECISION TIME!

Does this sound like you? If you have six or more of these traits, **Go to 1**

If not, start the adventure again and perhaps this time select other preferences you are drawn to.

The Helpful One

Congratulations you have reached Section 50.

You are nearly at the end of the Adventure!

Read the following list of personality traits and note which ones you agree with about your own character.

SUMMARY:

*Empathetic, sincere and warmhearted, sentimental

*Friendly, generous & Sometimes, self-sacrificing

*I can be very flattering

*Driven to be close to others

*Sometimes I don't acknowledge my own needs.

*Altruistic and unselfish

*I have a genuine love for others

*I don't want to feel unwanted

*I desire to feel that I am loved - it is important to me.

*People tell me I am a good host/hostess and I like to be appreciated

DECISION TIME!

Does this sound like you? If you have six or more of these traits, **Go to 2**

If not, start the adventure again and perhaps this time select other preferences you are drawn to.

The Striving for Success One

Congratulations you have reached Section 50.

You are nearly at the end of the Adventure!

Read the following list of personality traits and note which ones you agree with about your own character.

SUMMARY:

*Self-assured, I am told I am attractive and charming.

*Ambitious, competent and energetic

*Status conscious and highly driven; I care about image and what others think of me

*I can be quite competitive

*I am a good role model and can inspire others.

*I like doing worthwhile things

*I am a Professional

*I appreciate nice things

*I am motivated to distinguish oneself from others, to gain attention by being the best I can be

*I do not like failing at something.

DECISION TIME!

Does this sound like you? If you have six or more of these traits. **Go to 3**

If not, start the adventure again and perhaps this time select other preferences you are drawn to.

The I'm the Only One

Congratulations you have reached Section 50.

You are nearly at the end of the Adventure!

Read the following list of personality traits and note which ones you agree with about your own character.

SUMMARY:

*Self aware, sensitive and reserved

*I would call myself emotionally honest

*I can be quite self conscious

*I tend to steer away from ordinary ways of doing things and like my own space

*Sometimes I focus on my inner world quite a lot and focus on why I am so different

*I often think there is something inherently wrong with the world and worry about it

*I am creative at things I like to do though I often worry I am not good enough

*I feel motivated by true beauty

*I don't like people to intrude too much and sometimes I feel I must protect my feelings

*I vacillate between being overly involved or disinterested.

DECISION TIME!

Does this sound like you? If you have six or more of these traits. **Go to 4**

If not, start the adventure again and perhaps this time select other preferences you are drawn to.

The Thoughtful One

Congratulations you have reached Section 50.

You are nearly at the end of the Adventure!

Read the following list of personality traits and note which ones you agree with about your own character.

SUMMARY:

*Alert and curious, I concentrate on complexity

*Inventive but can be preoccupied

*Visionary but can be reclusive, preferring time to myself

*I like to feel I am a pioneer and innovator

*I don't like feeling I am incapable of something.

*I have a desire to be competent at whatever I am doing at the time.

*I like to solve problems.

*I am motivated to acquire knowledge and to understand my environment.

*I like to have things figured out.

*I don't like to feel under threat of something bad happening so I endeavor to be prepared.

DECISION TIME!

Does this sound like you? If you have six or more of these traits, **Go to 5**

If not, start the adventure again and perhaps this time select other preferences you are drawn to.

The Safe One

Congratulations you have reached Section 50.

You are nearly at the end of the Adventure!

Read the following list of personality traits and note which ones you agree with about your own character.

SUMMARY:

*Committed, security orientated

*Reliable and hardworking, responsible and trustworthy

*Quite cautious and can be indecisive

*I can be reactive and rebellious

*Hardworking Stability

*Stable and self reliant

courageously championing self and others

*I don't like feeling I don't have any support

*I like to feel secure and know what the future holds

*It is nice to have some security in life

*If I feel insecure I either get very animated and try to get a feeling of security back again or worry myself silly about it and hide away.

DECISION TIME!

Does this sound like you? If you have six or more of these traits, **Go to 6**

If not, start the adventure again and perhaps this time select other preferences you are drawn to.

The Fun One

Congratulations you have reached Section 50.

You are nearly at the end of the Adventure!

Read the following list of personality traits and note which ones you agree with about your own character.

SUMMARY:

*Extroverted and optimistic

*Versatile and spontaneous

*Playful and high spirited

*Often very practical

*There is a danger of me becoming exhausted as I often throw myself into enthusiasm

*Focused on worthwhile goals

*I don't like being tied down

*Freedom means a lot to me

*I don't like missing out

*Keeping preoccupied to avoid serious things.

DECISION TIME!

Does this sound like you? If you have six or more of these traits. **Go to 7**

If not, start the adventure again and perhaps this time select other preferences you are drawn to.

The War One

Congratulations you have reached Section 50.

You are nearly at the end of the Adventure!

Read the following list of personality traits and note which ones you agree with about your own character.

SUMMARY:

*Self confident, strong and assertive.

*Protective and resourceful.

*Can be magnanimous, with immense compassion.

*I do not like displays of weakness, though I shall fight for and defend the less fortunate.

*Self mastering and heroic at times.

*Do not like to be harmed or controlled by others.

*I have a desire to be in charge of the unpredictable in life.

*I am motivated to display my strength when threatened.

*I like to be important and dominate the environment as I prefer to stay in charge of what happens to me as much as possible.

*Justice and honoring truth mean a lot to me.

DECISION TIME!

Does this sound like you? If you have six or more of these traits, **Go to 8**

If not, start the adventure again and perhaps this time select other preferences you are drawn to.

The Peace One

Congratulations you have reached Section 50.

You are nearly at the end of the Adventure!

Read the following list of personality traits and note which ones you agree with about your own character.

SUMMARY:

*I am generally very accepting, trusting and stable. *Creative, optimistic and supportive of others - often putting others before myself and not good at asking for help myself.

*Sometimes too willing to go along with others to keep the peace.

*I am considered to be optimistic and I like everyone to get along - it disturbs me when they don't.

*I can be Indomitable and all embracing, bring people together and healing conflicts.

*I don't like to experience falling out with others and so do not give others cause for upset.

*People tell me I'm usually very calm - placid some say.

*I like peace and quiet though thrive on excitement too.

*It takes a great deal to make me angry, though when I reach that point I am steadfast and stoic.

*I am often the one who brings harmony and gets others to make up after arguments and fall outs.

DECISION TIME!

Does this sound like you? If you have six or more of these traits. **Go to 9**

If not, start the adventure again and perhaps this time select other preferences you are drawn to.

The imprint of your soul
Kitching   Whittaker   Enneagram

Each one of us creates our own reality through the lens of our personality. This concept essentially means that your reality, good or bad, is your creation. This is true for your outer reality, such as relationships and career, as well as your inner reality such as your health and your psychological wellbeing. So, the bad news is, this is all your fault. The good news is, we can fix this!

For those of you that know the essentials of Enneagram, you will recognise some familiar topics coming up, though the Kitching Whittaker approach and its unique typing system will be refreshing new material to enhance your knowledge. Certainly, there is new, never before seen, material for you here to supplement your knowledge.

For those who are new to the Kitching Whittaker Enneagram, be prepared for a treat too, as your authors and trainers with a collective sixty years of experience, have a reputation for presenting highly complex ideas in an accessible and entertaining manner, adding their own unique style and method of interpretation to empower your life.

Chapter 3: What Is Enneagram?

The Enneagram is a system of nine personality types based on the combination of modern psychology and traditional methodologies. This tool is not only useful for understanding ourselves but for understanding the other people in our lives as well. It has three major applications and they are:

●Personal growth and spiritual development

●Leadership skills development including team building and communication skills in business applications

●Success in personal and professional relationships

This system allows you to work more effectively in these areas because it allows you to increase your self-awareness and therefore, your emotional intelligence as you engage yourself and your environment. You are no longer ruled by emotions or patterns of thinking that affect your mood and therefore, the way you behave. Increased emotional intelligence allows you to build successful relationships with friends and family, and in your professional environment. This intelligence also allows you to support your character strengths and identify the qualities which are weaker and need development.

Before we delve into the history of the Enneagram, let's dive deeper into what it truly is and why it has survived centuries and is still so effective.

What Is Enneagram?

Enneagream is also called the Enneagram of Personality. The word Enneagram is derived from the Greek words ἐΝΝΈΑ (ennéa), which means "nine" and γράμμα (grámma), which means something "written" or "drawn." The Enneagram is based on a model of the human psyche with a foundation of understanding the typology of nine interconnected personality types. These nine personality types are represented by the diagram below.

At first glance, the structure of the Enneagram can seem quite confusing and intimidating. However, on closer examination, it can be seen that the structure is simple. The nine points are of equal distance apart along the circumference of the circle and each is designated a number from 1 to 9 with 9 at the top. Each point represents one of the nine personality types and each is interrelated with the other in specific ways. This interaction is indicated by the inner lines of the structure.

The nine personality types in numeric order are:

The Reformer

The Helper

The Performer

The Artist

The Observer

The Loyalist

The Enthusiast

The Protector

The Peacemaker

What is a Personality Type?

A personality type is a psychological classification of different types of individuals so that personality traits can be distinguished. These traits usually occur together consistently, especially when they conform to a certain pattern of responses.

For example, introverts and extroverts are two fundamentally different categories of people due to the traits they exhibit. However, introverts and extroverts are part of a continuous dimension, with many people falling in the middle of the spectrum.

Personality traits fall into one of the following 5 categories:

●Openness. This is also called openness to experience and people who register high in this trait are highly adventurous, love new experiences, and are curious. People who are very open often live by the philosophy that "Variety is the spice of life." On the other hand, people who register low in openness are the opposite and prefer to stick to their habits and avoid new experiences.

●Conscientiousness. Conscientious people are very organized and have a great sense of duty. These people are very goal-oriented and disciplined. To sum it up, conscientious people are planners and very dependable. People who are low in conscientiousness are more spontaneous and carefree in the way that they live.

●Extraversion. This trait speaks to how outgoing a person is. People who register high in extraversion are called extroverts and are what you might call the social butterflies in group settings. They draw energy from being in a crowd and are very chatty and assertive in social interactions. People who register low in extraversion are called introverts and prefer to be alone most of the time because their brains find it very difficult to process social interactions. Their energy gets depleted by being in large groups. Introvertism is often confused with shyness. However, shyness is a fear of social interaction.

●Agreeableness. This is a measure of how approachable a person is. A person who is high in agreeableness is often kind, warm, compassionate, and helpful towards others. Other people find it easy to trust such a person. People who are disagreeable are not as easily approached because they are less likely to cooperate. Disagreeable people often find other people suspicious and are often cold in their demeanor.

●Neuroticism. Neurotic characters are people who often obsess over things and display high levels of anxiety. Neurotic people often suffer from depression. On the other hand, people who score low in neuroticism are more emotionally stable, worry less, and tend to be less anxious.

The History of Enneagram

The origin of the Enneagram is unclear, and there are many theories as to where its roots came from. Despite the disputes of the origin of the Enneagram, all the theories seem connected through spirituality and specific mathematical and philosophical traditions.

Here are the theories that try to explain the origin of the Enneagram:

●Some historians believe that the Enneagram was part of the Pythagorian culture and dates back to over 4,000 years. This theory is supported by variations of the Enneagram symbol which supported sacred geometry back then. This line of mathematical thinking was passed on through Pluto, his disciple Plotinus and other neo-Platonists. They speak of nine divine qualities that manifest themselves in human nature.

●Others believe that this system came into the esoteric Judaism through the Jewish neo-Platonist philosopher called Philo because it appears as the Tree of Life in the ancient text for the symbol of nine foldness. This ancient text is called the Kabbalah.

●There are other speculations that the symbol appeared in Islam Sufi traditions as it was referenced in the Naqshbandi Order, also known as the Brotherhood of the Bees.

●The possibility of the Enneagram having esoteric Christianity roots has been discussed because of medieval references to the Evagrius' catalogue of various forms of temptation called Logismoi. This was later translated into the seven deadly sins.

●Ramon Llull (1232-1315) was a mathematician, polymath, philosopher, logician, Franciscan tertiary, and writer from the Kingdom of Majorca. He tried to integrate the different faith traditions using a philosophy and theology of nine principles.

●In the 17th century, an Enneagram-like drawing was found in the literature created by the Jesuit mathematician Athanasius Kircher.

In more recent times, Russian teacher, George Gurdjieff (1879-1949) used the Enneagram system to explain the laws evolving around the creation of the universe. The roots of this theory are much clearer compared to the others and Gurdjieff called it a symbol of Perpetual Motion. Gurdjieff mentioned that he was introduced to the Enneagram in the 1920s after he visited a monastery in Afghanistan.

Bolivian-born founder of the Arica School, which was established in 1968 in South America, Oscar Ichazo, also taught the Enneagram. His theories and teachings on the Enneagram of Personality formed part of a larger body of work which he called Protoanalysis. He exposed this work to a Chilean psychiatrist named Claudio Naranjo and through their efforts the Enneagram became part of modern psychological traditions. Also, through the efforts of persons like Bob Ochs, who studied with Naranjo, the Enneagram was introduced to several Christian communities in the United States. The system gained much more exposure through the writings of authors like Don Riso, who was the head of the Enneagram research and study in New York City and who wrote the book, "THE WISDOM OF THE ENNEAGRAM: THE COMPLETE GUIDE TO PSYCHOLOGICAL AND SPIRITUAL GROWTH FOR THE NINE PERSONALITY TYPES," which is co-written by Russo Hudson. Other famous authors that wrote on the subject of the Enneagram are David

Daniels, Jerry Wagner, Mark Bodnarczuk, Sandra Maitri, Beatrice Chestnut, and Ginger Lapid-Bogda.

Ever since it has been put into the spotlight like this, the Enneagram has been validated through experimental and empirical studies. It has also been cross-referenced with other constructs of psychology such as the MBTI, which stands for Myers-Briggs Type Indicator. The MBTI is a system of taking personality inventory through an introspective self-report questionnaire. The results of this questionnaire allows an individual to discover the differing psychological preferences in how he or she perceives the world around them and make decisions based on those observations. The MBTI was constructed by Katharine Cook Briggs (1875–1968) and her daughter Isabel Briggs Myers (1897–1980) and was based on the conceptual theories of the Swiss psychiatrist, Carl Jung (1875–1961).

Using the Enneagram for Self-Understanding and Discovery

As mentioned earlier, the Enneagram describes nine distinct personality types. Each personality type is characterized by distinct mental and emotional traits. These mental and emotional characteristics help define the way the owner of the personality type thinks and feels. This therefore, influences the life experiences that this personal will have.

Personality types are so important that they have defined the persona that we carry throughout our lives. This personality type defines the way that a person thinks and feels about him or herself, how he represents him or herself to the world, and how he or she perceives the world around them. In essence, your personality type is your true-self and is a description of the inner landscape that shapes you.

Personality type and personality are two terms that are not to be confused. While your personality type is a fixed condition, your personality, which is also called your ego, is conditional and changes with your environment. Since our environments are always changing, so do our personalities. Your personality type however remains grounded no matter what you go through, who you meet, or what day it is.

This is important because it shows that no matter how much your environment changes or how much you grow and evolve as a person, the center of who you are as a person remains the same. This knowledge allows you to gain confidence as you embark on a journey of self-awareness and self-discovery. You will know that who you are today will fundamentally not be different tomorrow or any other day no matter what life experiences you go through.

Also, knowing your personality type can help steer you in the right direction to discover your strengths and weaknesses, the things that make you feel happy and fulfilled, and knowing how you can strengthen your weaknesses.

Understanding your personality type is not so that you can be forced into a mold. Instead, it is a useful tool for better understanding yourself and how you relate to other people. With this understanding, you can approach the journey to self-discovery knowing that your traits that need to be reformed can be done and that you can strengthen those that make you a great individual for others to be around. This will ultimately make you a happier person who is mentally stable. With mental stability comes the increased likelihood of better physical health.

How the Enneagram Can Help You Develop Your Relationships

The Enneagram is not only founded on psychology but is a means to deeper spiritual understanding of one's self. This system can be a source of insight into your mind, heart, and soul so that you can gain the wisdom to make good life choices that can enrich you as an individual and enrich the relationships that you form with other people. Knowing your personality type can help you become a more effective communicator and communication is at the heart of every relationship that your form, whether it be personal or professional.

Communication involves the exchange of information between two or more persons. However, communication is not just about what is written or said. Often times, it is what we do not say that has the most impact on how effective communication is. Our body language and how our spirits interact has a big part to play in how we transmit and receive information from each other. The Enneagram allows you to gain greater insight into why and how you communicate with other people. This knowledge can allow you to develop strategic approaches to the way that you seek out and interact with other people so that you can act in a manner that is most effective when it comes to imparting to your feelings, ideas, and thoughts to others.

The Enneagram allows you to also understand how you influence others so that you can adjust your communication style to suit your audience and even increase your circle of influence. This can help you become a more effective leader because you understand the different needs of the people around you and you understand your strengths as well as theirs. This allows you to empower yourself and to nourish growth and performance. Part of being a good leader also involves strategic thinking and decision-making. By being aware of your personality type, you can be more aware of your core motivations and what drives you to increase the quality of your life and those around you.

All of this helps you develop a character of finesse. Since you have this insight into the character of others, you can better anticipate their reactions and approach communication in a way that keeps the interaction as friendly and as insightful as possible.

At the core of it all, building better communication skills helps you build stronger, long-lasting relationships with not only yourself but with your friends, family, colleagues, and others. This encourages skills of objectivity and compassion so that you can not only draw out your own strength but those of the people that surround you. Gaining insight into the Enneagram makes this process a lot easier and faster for you.

Chapter 4: Center Yourself

The Centers represent the various types and relationships

between similarities and differences of each. Basically,

these concerns orbit a dominant, quite unconscious,

expressive reaction to disconnection with the center of

the self. The Inherent center embodies RAGE while the Emotional hub feels SHAME.

The Intellectual Center gives us FEAR. All nine types contain these emotional states,

but in each Center, the behaviors of the types are mainly affected by that Center's theme.

The emotion in each center determines what coping mechanisms our person uses.

What does that mean exactly? We will now discover the types by the emotions that guide them and how that shapes us individually.

A. The Inherent - Rage

Eights, Nines and Ones have that "gut feeling" process nailed down. They are led by the body, often seek justice and social status. The Boss (8) will make it easy for you to know they are angry! They may raise their voice or move and do not feel the need to get permission for their behavior. Our Mediator (9) will do everything to remain in denial about their anger. The Perfectionist (1) are notorious for repressing fury. Instead, they focus on relationships and their surroundings, pouring their negative energy into building their ego.

These intellectual people are part of our everyday life. You can surely think of someone in school who always stood up for what was right. It is quite easy to remember someone that consistently provided a safe place for others to get along.

You can focus on the negative in life, or you can focus on the positive and act on those feelings. The Inherent is trained at breeding positivity.

B. The Emotional – Shame

Twos, Threes, and Fours crave positive energy, so they feel appreciated. It's a simple concept that allows them to control their feelings of shame. For instance,

The Assistant (2) will do whatever they can to convince anyone they are good people. The longer they feel loved, the shorter their experiences of shame will be.

The Doer (3) are self-explanatory. Their actions speak louder than anything, and they will act convince others that they are respectable, caring individuals. The Eccentric (4) focus on their amazing gifts of creativity and abilities and overshadow any shame they may feel.

Our Emotional individuals help keep our eyes on the best that life has to offer.

Should a dismal situation arise, you can count on The Emotionals to make an

alternate, positive solution available that they are proud of.

C. The Intellectual – Fear

Fives, Sixes, and Sevens will give you a systematic look at a problem. The

Observers (5) value their privacy and strive to be self-sufficient. Their energy is

concentrated on understanding our world on their terms in hopes of participating

with confidence. However, they tend to keep themselves busy with their private,

complex worlds. The Loyal Skeptic (6) is like a beehive. They are full of anxiety

and just want security and work on finding it in lots of ways such as financial,

spiritual and professional. The Epicure (7) brings excitement to fear by keeping

busy with different, stimulating projects. They will avoid hurt, defeat, and deprivation even if that means procrastinating.

Our lovely Intellectuals are our best analysts. You can depend on them to look at

every angle and give a confident answer because of their fear of inadequacy. You

are safe in their capable hands.

D. Fly High

It is possible to score high on different types in the same Center because they

share personality traits and behaviors. To understand each other, we should

realize that The Wing bears an influence. The Wing refers to the personality type

on each side of our dominant type. For instance, if you score as an Perfectionist

(1), you will strongly relate to The Assistant (2) as well as The Mediator (9).

Some mature individuals may develop what is referred to as a Second Wing. This

is especially true for those seeking therapeutic or spiritual work. This could be due to our elders understanding more about life, our world and their place in the

equation. It is safe to say that being aware of your type is only the beginning.

There is so much more to understanding The Enneagram than just a number or

an illustration with a circle and points with lines going every direction. Our

human body develops in stages; such is true with our psyche.

Chapter 5: Personality Test… Identify

Your Personality Type

There are many personality tests available online or in published material. This book is not designed to suggest one test over another. Instead, I suggest that you select the one that you feel the most comfortable with, as long as it is reputable. Some of the tests online are free and others charge a small fee.

While filling out the personality test and getting a better idea of your personality type is only a small portion of your journey towards a significant personal transformation, it is a very important step. It will help guide you towards your ultimate goal.

Below, I will suggest a few web addresses that you can explore at your leisure to find the personality test that suits you. Also, you can find an example of a personality type test in the Annex. You can even decide to complete more than one personality test to see if the results are similar. What matters most is to answer these questions truthfully. There are no right or wrong answers, just make sure that you are honest and sincere. You are not trying to get hired for a job or to please anyone. The purpose of this test is to help you. So, you owe it to yourself to be honest and to take this test as seriously as possible, so the results can be accurate. Only in this way will you then have a solid basis from which to build.

Keep in mind that you might be surprised by the results. Sometimes people have a perception of themselves that is not accurate. You might think you are a very daring person, when in fact, you really seek security. You also might think you have been a follower all your life, when truly you have been leading the way for others. This is another reason why personality tests are so helpful. They are like special mirrors you've never accessed before, because you never knew about them.

Chapter 6: The Enneagram Types

Now that we have had an introduction to the history of the Enneagram and a brief look into its origins and how widespread it is, we will now take an in-depth analysis into the nine Enneatypes that make up the Enneagram, and how the system works as a whole.

The Enneagram itself is the visual representation of the nine **Enneatypes**. Every single person is considered to have a **single dominant Enneatype**. Other types can influence someone's personality, which we will examine in much greater detail when we discuss **Wings** and **Instinctual Subtypes**, but each of the nine Enneatypes is something akin to a category, and every individual falls into one of them.

One question which often gets debated is whether an individual's Enneatype is determined prior or after to birth. The reality is that there's no consensus in the scientific and spiritual communities about this matter. From one hand an Enneatype may be determined **prior** to birth (implying a genetic pre-determination). From another hand it may be something acquired in early life – through learning and experience. This, of course, by and large is the great Nature vs Nurture debate, and the Enneagram system is no stranger to it. However, for our purposes here in this book, the determination of one's Enneatype is not important. What is important though, is knowing the **nature** and **differences** of the nine types, **how to interact** with each, and **how to determine which type we are**. This is what we will spend the next several sections on.

There is also another important aspect of understanding the Enneatypes. While it can be very important to understand which type we are, and how to identify Enneatype characteristics in other people, it's also very important to remember that **everyone is different**, and anyone can have **similarities and differences** from others. Two people with different

Enneatypes may have almost **as many things in common** as two people of the **same type**. With this I would like to state that knowing someone else's Enneatype should **never** be a reason to pre-judge or stereotype others. In fact, there's **never** a good reason to pre-judge or stereotype others. And which Enneatype someone belongs to is never ever a determination of whether someone is a good person or a bad person. Only **getting to know** someone can tell you that.

On the other hand, learning about your own Enneatype can be one of the best and most important ways to understand more about yourself, and what you can do to excel and develop, as an individual, as a partner, or as a member of a team. The best way to identify which type you are (and that is what I advice!) is to simply read each of the following sections and take note of which Enneatype you identify with most. Please, be honest with yourself when assessing which type you are, as misaligning yourself with the incorrect Enneatype may do far more harm to your personal growth and development than good.

Alternatively, if you would like a more immediate result – there are many "complete" solutions out there which can test your closeness to each Enneatype. These tests vary in terms of their length and perceived depth of uncovering your Enneatype. Just to name a few: **The Essential Enneagram Test by David Daniels**, **The Wagner Enneagram Personality Style Scales by Jerome P. Wagner**, **The Riso-Hudson Enneagram Type Indicator by Don Riso and Russ Hudson**.

There are also many short personality tests out there, which promise to identify your Enneatype literally in 5-7 minutes (for instance, **enneagramtest.net**). However, as I mentioned above my recommendation would be to start with learning about the Enneatypes first and only then try to define which Enneatype you may belong to. This will help you avoid "locking" yourself into a particular Enneatype due to a very fast and potentially unreliable "quick" online Enneagram test.

Finally, remember too that each of the following Enneatypes, one through nine, are always associated with their corresponding number. That's why, when referring to various Enneatypes, I will be also using numbers as the Enneatype indicator.

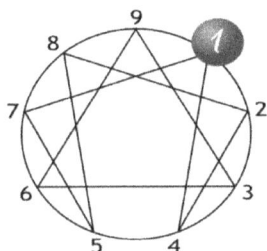

Enneagram Type 1: The Reformer

The **Reformer** is a perfectionist. Someone who is very responsible, and intensely fixated on improvement, whether personal or of the things around them. Essentially, these are people who are always striving to make everything better. A Reformer may give off the impression that nothing is ever quite good enough. Everything could always be just that much better.

Such tendency gives them a reputation of being a perfectionist, or some might even say an idealist—someone who is ever seeking to bring order to the chaotic world around them, someone who wants to improve, someone who wants to, well, reform.

Reformers have a very keen eye for detail. They tend to be acutely aware of the flaws that they possess within themselves, hence the constant desire for self-improvement. At the same time, they tend to also be very quick to see flaws in other people as well as in the various situations that they may find themselves in.

The constant pressure of what feels to them like inadequacies or flaws is what fuels their ever-raging zeal for improvement. This, of course, can be a great benefit to themselves and others, as their drive for perfection can help carry others who may be falling behind, but

Reformers must always be aware of the effect of their drive for perfection on those around them. And as for those non-Type One's who regularly interact with Reformers it is very important to remember that their perfectionism isn't directed at you, but rather at a situation or scenario.

A Type One may have trouble always achieve what they see to be perfection, and therefore One's have a strong tendency to be very hard on themselves, and feel highly inadequate, feeling as though they have always fallen short. While they tend to always strive for improvement, they also tend to only see what they have not accomplished, rather than appreciating what they have. This often has the effect of causing Reformers to be frequently angry, as anger is all too often a byproduct of guilt and misplaced resentment. While a Reformer will often be very hard on themselves and often quite angry with themselves, they can also direct their anger at others for not meeting up to their standards, or to the world in general for being such a cesspool of imperfection (in their eyes, of course, whether it's true or not is up for debate).

It's important to note however, that anger is a negative quality, and due to the Reformer's nature as a perfectionist, they will quite often think of anger as a quality that must be repressed or eliminated. So while a One may deal with anger issues, that does not mean that they will be an outwardly angry person, but rather they may have deep internal anger at themselves. Thus it is important to treat One's with empathy and understanding, being aware that they may be suffering internally.

Finally, if you are a Reformer, remember to **take a break** once in a while! One's are often workaholics who never quit until they get the job done.

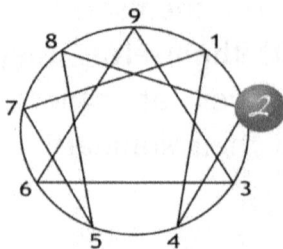

Enneagram Type 2: The Helper

A person with the personality type of the **Helper** is exactly what they sound like, a helper. A person who wants to help others, and feel that they need to be needed.

Helper's generate their own self-worth from helping others. Their deepest held value is being there for those who need it. Their most lofty ideal is that of love, and their most honorable duty is that of selflessness. In a Two's eyes, the entire purpose for existence is to **give to others**. Helpers tend to be very active and involved in their community. They also tend to be highly aware socially. A Two is generally very extroverted and sociable. They will never forget your birthday, or anyone else's. And they will almost always go above and beyond to be there in a pinch for a friend, partner, or team member.

Helper's tend to be very in tune with their emotions, and they are certainly not afraid of their emotions. They are warm and caring people can care very much about all of their personal relationships, whether friendly, romantic, or otherwise. They tend to devote a great percentage of their time and energy to their relationships, but they also often expect to be recognized and appreciated by those individuals in those relationships for the efforts that they put into them.

A lot of a Helper's personal identity and self-worth are frequently derived from what they perceive to be their level of ability to help others. In order for them to feel good, they need their loved ones to feel good. They feel important when a loved one comes to them for help, guidance or advice. Virtue and selflessness are things that make a Helper feel complete and whole.

If you identify as a Helper, you must be very cautious of your own needs, and make sure that you are not neglecting yourself in favor of helping others. Constantly being available for others can be very exhausting, and it can lead to emotional issues such as poorly controlled mood swings, and can even have physical effects. It is not uncommon for Helpers to simply burn out. Self-care is vitally important for Helpers. It is crucial for them to understand that it is virtually impossible for someone to completely be available to others if they are not taking care of themselves and ensure a healthy balanced life, emotionally and physically.

For those with loved ones who are Helpers, the most important thing to remember is to give back. You must not take advantage of a Helper's nature. That is their primary vulnerability and to exploit it would be the lowest form of malice. You can help Helpers by accepting their help and acknowledging their assistance. Never forget to remind them of how much you need them and how much you appreciate their help and support. Ultimately, a Helper is all about support, so just make sure that you are supporting the supporter as much as you can, and everyone will be better.

Helpers are some of the most special and delicate souls around, and they can't do what they're made to do without the rest of us allowing them to.

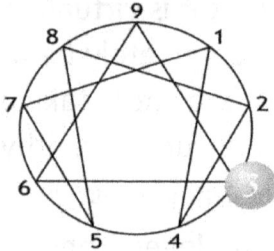

Enneagram Type 3: The Achiever

The third Enneagram type is that of the **Achiever**. Achievers are people who are highly attuned to the presentation of success. They frequently strive to attain validation in their lives and actions.

A major aspect of the lives of Type Threes is the need to **feel validated for them to feel worthy**. An Achiever wants to be admired, they need to succeed. Threes are often very hard working individuals, and they also tend to be extremely competitive, and intensely focused on the pursuit of their goals. These are people who are relentless in their pursuit of success. Nothing is good enough unless it's the best. A successful career doesn't mean anything unless they are at the top of their firm, for example. Or being attractive isn't good enough unless they are more attractive than everyone else.

Achievers often think of themselves as being self-made, regardless of how accurate that assessment actually is. It is very common for a Three to find a field of expertise or area of practice that they do in fact excel at, as without the validation they receive from excelling in that particular field, they would have a very difficult time indeed. Their need for validation via success and achievement is so complete that it may even come across as desperate.

Achievers tend to be very extroverted, socially competent and in many cases undeniably charismatic. They have an ability to present themselves to appear the way they want to, and they are usually very self-confident and highly driven. Their practicality may border on pragmatism, and may even go as far as being ethically questionable. However, Threes also tend to be very energetic, and their excitement and energy can often rub off on others they associate with. In fact, the concept of "friends" and "associates" can be somewhat blurred for Achievers as their zeal and charisma tend to make them excellent networkers and employees, able to take advantage of the way people respond to them in order to advance themselves in their careers, or socially.

Achievers should be very careful with confusing real happiness, with the kind of false happiness that is dangled like a carrot in front of them by our culture and the constructs of our society. It is crucial that a Three look inward and discover what real success means to them. While society may tell you that wealth and a strikingly attractive partner are what success is, that may not be what you actually need in your life to feel fulfilled. If you are an Achiever, get in tune with what really makes you happy, and make that the target of your goals.

Intimacy is often very challenging for Threes. The deep-seated need for validation can be very detrimental to an Achievers' self-image, regardless of how they present themselves, and it can be very easy for them to be internally overwhelmed with shame and fear. If you have a loved one who is a Three, make sure you always bear in mind what they may be feeling inside, even if they are not always forthcoming about it, and make sure to help them see what real success really is.

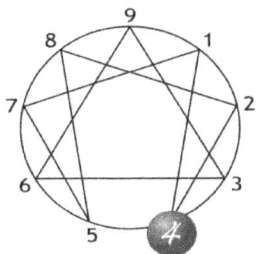

Enneagram Type 4: The Individualist

The **Individualist** is a person who feels somehow different or unique. Quite often, this may be due to a Four's feeling of a lack of true identify, resulting in identity seeking behavior.

Fours are often people who tend to construct their personal identity around the idea of being in some way **outside of the mainstream**; as being some kind of a fringe element. They are not just people who conduct themselves in an individualistic way, they are people who are actively and self-consciously individualistic.

Self-perception can certainly vary of Individualist to Individualist, but they may often see their individuality as either a gift or a curse; and quite often a combination of both. The idea of being outside of regular society, set apart from the common masses, is highly appealing to a Four, but such a personality can also lead Individualists to feel that they are missing out on the fun and social comfort of the 'commoners' that they so desire to be apart from.

This often confusing set of conflicting feelings can lead to a Four feeling like they are in some ways better, or superior, to the common population, while at the same time secretly feeling envious of others, or simply like they just **don't belong**. Fours are sometimes plagued with feelings of wanting to fit in with others, but at the same time harboring a deep fear that achieving increased social acceptance will somehow diminish their individuality, the quality they hold most dear. These mixed and conflicting feelings can be quite painful for the Individualist and may be associated with intense feelings of shame and fear.

Individualists tend to be very sensitive emotionally, as well as being not just emotionally deep, but emotionally complex. There is a lot of internal conflict in Fours. They often see being misunderstood and ignored as part of their identity and something to protect, while at the same time feeling unappreciated and undervalued for the exact same reasons. Individualists often come across as being temperamental or moody, and it is not at all uncommon for a Four to simply retreat from the world when they are faced with circumstances they feel they can't handle.

Fours tend also to be very internal in nature, whether intellectual or emotionally inclined, they tend to internalize things and be highly reflective. Much of an Individualist's frustrations may come from a feeling of not being able to express or articulate the things they feel inside, and thus, Fours are very often inclined toward the arts. And even if a Four doesn't pursue the arts, they frequently tend to have a good appreciation for art and often feel that they have excellent taste.

If you have an Individualist loved one, the most important thing to remember is to **listen** and to encourage them to **always express themselves**. It is very easy for an Individualist to fall into the trap of fantasizing about better conditions rather than acting, so try to encourage a Four's loved one to action.

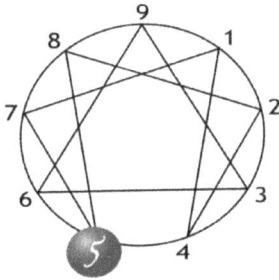

Enneagram Type 5: The Investigator

Investigators are people who spend a lot of time thinking. They tend to stand at a figurative distance and observe. They tend to feel as if they do not possess the inner strength necessary to face their life, and as a result they have a tendency to withdraw into themselves, and to retreat to the perceived safety of their mind, where they can prepare themselves mentally for all of the challenges the world can offer up to them.

Fives are very comfortable with their thoughts and feel at home in the realm of their minds. They are almost always highly intelligent. Investigators tend to read quite a lot and often eschew fiction and entertainment that they may consider being either beneath them or a distraction that takes them away from learning or improving their mind. Fives are also generally very thoughtful people and enjoy engaging in deep, meaningful conversation when in situations in which they feel comfortable.

An Investigator's interests often lie in science, but it's equally likely that a Five may find themselves interested in the arts and in the humanities. In any case, it is highly likely that a Five will find an area of particular interest and become an expert in that field.

It is certainly not uncommon for Fives to be a little bit on the eccentric side. They don't very often feel any need or desire to alter their worldview in order to align with the majority. They can be a little bit like the Individualist in that regard.

An issue that Fives often have, however, is that while they have a high level of comfort within their own thoughts, they are rarely as comfortable in public or in a social setting. As a result, it is common for Fives to have a hard time dealing with and expressing their emotions. They may also find it hard to meet the needs of a partner in a relationship. Generally speaking, Fives have a tendency to be very shy individuals, who are so non-intrusive and non-confrontational that they even have a hard time asking for help, even if they have a loved one who would be more than willing to do so.

Investigators often take on a persona of aloofness or of intellectual arrogance. This is generally for the purpose of compensating for feelings of inadequacy or not feeling properly equipped to deal with the world, but as a result, this often leads to distant interpersonal relationships and a lack of real intimacy in their lives.

However, it is worth it to work through this with Fives, as once they become comfortable with someone, they can often be counted on as a great companion and life-long friend.

Investigators should strive to be open with their emotions and with others. It may be hard to trust others, but once someone earns that trust, deep, meaningful and truly important relationships can come from it.

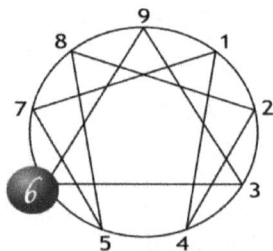

Enneagram Type 6: The Loyalist

The personality of a **Loyalist** can be boiled down to one thing: **a conflict between trust and mistrust**. A frequent feeling of Sixes is insecurity. They often feel like they never really have steady footing. In short, a person with the Type Six personality is someone who is largely controlled by fear and anxiety.

The anxiety that a Six experiences may have any number of root causes, and as such can be very difficult to thoroughly describe or define, but the general quality that Sixes tend to have in common is a personality in which fear plays a major role and tends to sit front and center in their hearts and minds. These fears can manifest in the form of a generally worrying type of attitude, and Sixes also have a tendency to constantly think about, almost fantasize about, all of the things that could go wrong in any given scenario.

While this tendency certainly does have its advantages — Loyalists make excellent troubleshooters, for example — it also has the effect of depriving Sixes of the peace of mind that they often so desperately need, and they also tend to lack spontaneity, as any unknown or unfamiliar act or action is met with a flood of negative, intrusive thoughts regarding the safety or success of said act or action.

This type of anxiety and fear is what is often referred to as 'defensive suspiciousness' and it is rooted in the Loyalist's feelings of being poorly equipped to defend against the many challenges and dangers the world could potentially throw at us. This, naturally, results in a personality that is very slow to trust, but on the flip side, once that trust is earned and achieved, it is nearly unshakable. Even that though can have a downside, and a Loyalist may end up extending their trust far beyond what has been actually earned.

Loyalists often just feel like they need someone or something to believe in. Thus, Sixes can frequently have a strange relationship with authority. While their distrusting nature often will lead them to reject or even actively distrust authority, they can also somewhat counterintuitively tend to be drawn toward external sources of authority, whether that be spiritual, individual or political. While a Six is generally more likely to reject institutions like religions, law enforcement, or governments, they may be inclined to fall into smaller, insidious organizations that are designed to pray on people like them and others.

In either case, Loyalists are generally not actively aware that their actions and intentions are often driven by fear, and it could be very helpful for them or their loved ones to examine that and help find that understanding. Anxiety and fear can be a constant presence for Sixes, which means that it is very possible that they have no idea how anxiety is affecting their everyday choices and decisions. The loved ones of Sixes can help immensely by working through their anxieties with them and helping them see that their actions are often reactive to their background anxiety rather than being autonomous choices.

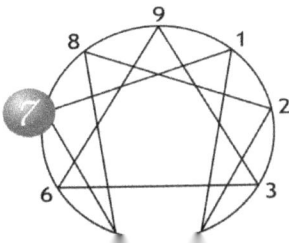

Enneagram Type 7: The Enthusiast

Enthusiasts tend to be well planned, pleasure seekers, who seem to be always looking for a distraction.

Sevens are the type of person who is always very concerned about doing things, taking action, having fun, living an adventure. They tend to be very forward thinking and focus on their future. They tend to be rather restless and often feel as though the next big thing is just around the corner. They also tend to be very quick thinking, love making all of the plans for themselves and others, and generally have lots and lots of energy. Enthusiasts are creative and open-minded, they tend to have lots of talents, and naturally, they are generally very much extroverted. The enthusiasm from which their name is derived manifests in the form of never believing in any kind of self-denial, and enjoying every sensual pleasure the world has to offer.

Enthusiasts are generally very practical and highly skilled people. They are often very good at self-promotion, self-marketing and working a crowd to get what they want. It is not at all uncommon for an Enthusiast to have an entrepreneurial passion, and they can generally drum up as much enthusiasm among others for a project, plan or endeavor. Enthusiasts tend to be most successful when they are afforded the opportunity to hone their skills and focus on a particular talent. However, having said that, focusing on one thing in particular is not always an easy task for an Enthusiast. An attitude of always waiting for the 'next big thing' can have the effect of diluting a Seven's efforts and dividing their attention from the task at hand.

One of the biggest potential problems for an Enthusiast is that they often pursue pleasure as a compulsion. It can be an overpowering force, rather than a well-executed plan. Sevens also tend to be afraid of negative thoughts and states of mind, which can be pushed away by always filling up their attention with distractions. As such, Enthusiasts are very often multi-taskers who are always inclined to keep their options open, and by constantly seeking stimulation. Because of this tendency, Enthusiasts must be very careful, as they are highly prone to addiction, whether it's substance abuse, shopping, gambling, or sexual in nature.

Sevens often tend to hold themselves in a relatively high esteem, and highly value their own talents. You'll often find an Enthusiast playing down their shortcomings and frequent vices in favor of their strengths and good qualities. They may also have strong feelings of entitlement and have a tendency toward being self-centered and egotistical. Because of the fact that Sevens very frequently avoid confronting their darker and more painful emotions, it's not uncommon for them to be poor empathizers, never truly acknowledging or understanding the suffering and pain of others.

It's important to always encourage a Seven's creativity. This will help Enthusiasts stay focused on their natural optimistic qualities, making them feel satisfied and fulfilled, which will naturally positively affect those who surround them.

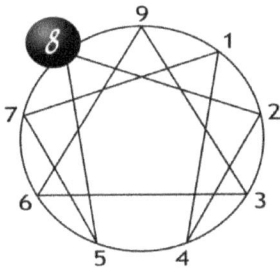

Enneagram Type 8: The Challenger

An Eight is a person who takes charge of a situation. Their compulsion to lead is less about controlling people, and more about a deep-seated aversion to being controlled by others.

Challengers are just what they sound like. They challenge authority, they cannot tolerate being controlled. And it's not just control by people they have an aversion to; a Challenger can no more abide being controlled by circumstance than they can by a person. A Challenge is the master of their own destiny; the only person who can determine their own fate.

An Eight may at times veer somewhat toward the more domineering aspect of their Ennea, as the most sensible way of avoiding all control, at least in the eyes of the Challenger, is to assert control over others. To a Challenger, the only way to truly and completely escape control is to exert control over everyone and everything. And while this tendency, in some cases an urge or even compulsion, can quickly spiral into serious conflict and problems, it should not be assumed that every Challenger is an overpowering, domineering individual. In many cases, an Eight simply understands their nature and why they experience the needs they feel, and they exercise them in a healthy way.

For example, when a Challenger recognizes that the needs and desire of their personality type have the potential to be harmful, even dangerous, they will often choose to exert their control over their own urges, keeping them in check. Those tendencies, however, will always remain there, just under the surface. So if an Eight wishes to retain control over their own urges, they must be ever-vigilant.

On the positive side, Challengers generally have very good and strong instincts, and they are usually quite well equipped mentally and emotionally, to set and follow their own path. They intend to get what they want out of life, which is as much as possible, and they have no problem acting on their intentions. Eights are fiercely independent, financially, spiritually, and ideologically, and they shun what they consider to be **'herd mentality'** at all cost. They never fall for populist lies, and they would never trust authority. They often may think of themselves as something of an outlaw, if not literally, then at least metaphorically.

Challengers also tend to exhibit very intense physical appetites, as well as being far less likely to experience guilt or shame, and therefore must be very deliberate about empathizing with others when satisfying their needs. Closely associated with these issues is a Challenger's general aversion to vulnerability, making intimate relationships difficult for them.

Challengers are usually healthiest mentally when they have made peace with the society in which they live. Whether that's achieving financial independence or home out in a rural area, a Challenger can find peace when they make peace with the world they live in and the people they love. When a Challenger finds this peace they will understand what true independence is.

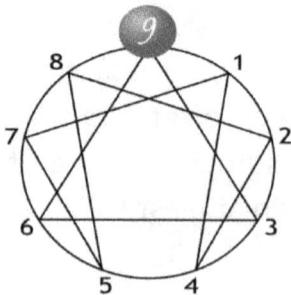

Enneagram Type 9: The Peacemaker

In the eyes of a Nine, their mission in life is to maintain peace and harmony and engender unity for all. **Peacemakers** avoid conflict if at all possible. It is very common for Peacemakers to be introverts, as in their view, the world is full of nothing but conflict, and the more you interact with it, the more opportunities for conflict arise. This may often lead to Nines being somewhat withdrawn and reclusive.

There certainly are Peacemakers who have very active and healthy social lives, but in all likelihood, those social interactions are psychically and mentally exhausting, and they will generally need to spend some time alone to 'recover', so to speak. However, contrary to popular wisdom, Nines are not generally anxious or stress-prone people. In fact, they tend to be rather easy going. After all, going with the figurative flow generates a good deal less conflict than challenging and questioning things. Nines tend to be very likable as they seek to make people happy and not rub anyone the wrong way. As humor is a great tension breaker, you'll often find that Peacemakers are also the ones who are quickest to crack a joke.

Peacemakers tend to be very trusting people. They see the best in others, they want the best for everyone, and they often truly believe in their hearts that everything will work out well. They are very optimistic people who always keep a positive attitude and worldview.

Nines can often exhibit an aversion to change. Change can feel like a form of conflict to a Peacemaker, so it can be very difficult for them to tolerate and accept. A Peacemaker often requires a figurative '**even keel**' in their life to feel comfortable and secure, and change is a major disruption to that stability. It is very important that Peacemakers do not fall into the trap of being unable to generate any motivation to take any action in their lives, and as a result become stagnant, unable to affect any positive change in their lives.

The irony here is that by the Nine's very nature, they are generally highly adaptable and very much capable of change. It's the motivation to change and acceptance of change that is challenging for the Peacemaker. Thus for those with loved ones who are Peacemakers, it's important to remember to **encourage and support** them to **accept the changes** that they need to. Remind them of times in the past when positive results came from change, and how easy it was in retrospect. This will help bolster the Peacemakers confidence to make the changes they need to make.

The biggest thing that Peacemakers tend to be guilty of is not giving themselves the credit they deserve. So remember to **commend and recognize** the good qualities and positive achievements of the Peacemakers, and remind them that you appreciate them. And if you are a Nine, reflect on what you have accomplished and how far you've come. You may surprise yourself.

Chapter 7: Type Two: The Heartfelt

Caregiver

In This Chapter:

Pleasing yourself while pleasing others
What are my needs?

Sunny on the outside—where are the clouds? Relating without helping

Learning to receive

Identifying the Two in yourself and others

Twos are sometimes difficult to detect. Women are often programmed to be givers, when it is not their core trait. True Twos go out of their way to give while hiding their own needs, but may become upset when others don't follow their advice or appreciate their attention. They generally show the positive side and don't reveal much of their pain and vulnerabilities. When they do, it is a big deal!

Nonverbal cues

Twos want to please, so they'll do anything to be the person needed in a particular situation, to the extent of forgetting what might be best for the others, as well as themselves. It is so automatic. Their self- worth is based on how well they please others.

In identifying Twos, look for: Smiles

Good eye contact Confidence in giving

Someone who's looking for hugs by giving hugs An affectionate nature

Someone dressed colorfully, cheerfully, and to please A seductive, inviting nature

Generosity, but sometimes too much

verbal cues

Twos offer advice, say positive things in flattering tones and talk in a cheery way. There can be a slightly forced tone to keep it positive, against a possible backdrop of pain or displeasure. More mature Twos are totally natural. Twos talk about love, giving, pleasure, and happiness. Their language is can-do, with an emphasis on the positive.

Other verbal cues:

Language to influence the listener.

Two's advice or suggestions are the only way to go. Twos speak about the bright side of life and avoid being negative except for when you get negative.

Tend to be extroverted, engaging, and personal. Expressions can seem planned or affected.

Twos in Caregiving

The Two's call is "Let me help you!" though the subtle underlying motivator is being able to say, "I made you happy!" Who could refuse such a giver, initially at least? Nurturing others is widely seen as a generous service, so the Two slides easily into the role, or so it seems. In an effort to be giving, Twos try to hide their own needs. Constant smiles may mask internal frustration. Understandably, they want to be appreciated for their giving, but acknowledgement isn't always forthcoming.

As a Two, you can be somewhat conflicted about being needed as you also want your own independence, but playing a role that is based solely on giving offers little in the way of independence. Some see it as unacceptable for a caregiver to have her own needs. But if your Loved One sometimes takes advantage of your good nature, wanting too much or being ungrateful for your giving (or over-giving), you may reach a limit. Suddenly you can't stand the neediness and demands, and may react by being punishing, or angrily setting limits.

It is a strange dance, isn't it? As a Two, you struggle to balance this back and forth between dependence on needing to be needed, and independence. When others aren't responsive, it is uncomfortable to feel that you need their response. It seems like a weakness. You feel strongest when others automatically need you. And if they praise you, well, then the sky is the limit. The dance continues.

Twos are more likely to be women, though there are plenty of Two men. Real Twos are almost incapable of dropping the caring, nurturing role. It may be difficult for others to move from a nurturing role, but Twos can be devastated when their Loved Ones no longer need them. Transitioning a Loved One from home to assisted living or a nursing home, or letting a sibling do the primary tasks, can be especially wrenching for a Two. Watching others care for the one you love can foster feelings of jealousy and rejection. You're being prevented from doing what you do best.

Two's Positive Traits

Twos are charming, a pleasure and a comfort as givers of caring and support. Their positive traits include being:

Uplifting - You focus on the glass half full. You love to delight others, particularly when you have a receptive and appreciative Loved One. Lovers of beauty, Twos will create the most attractive room for the Loved One.

Industrious - You work hard to alleviate excessive pain and make your Loved One feel great, look good, and be happy. You'll put in the necessary time and attention to plan the family holiday, make sure all goes smoothly, and greet everyone with a smile. You keep the energy up to produce a great result and point out everyone's best traits.

Empathic - You have the gift of empathy allowing you to tune in to your Loved One's needs and delight in her successes.

Acknowledging - You also care about promoting others who need to be recognized for their service, wanting them to feel good around you. The hospital or nursing home staff naturally takes to you.

Two's Challenges

Twos can at times feel possessive, jealous, controlling, and territorial. If you feel others are competing with you for your Loved One's love or loyalty, you'll do almost anything to win. "I am your giver, above others."

Lack of Self-awareness - You can be almost completely blind to your own needs. How, then, can you be truly present? How can your relationships be authentic if you yourself are absent?

False Front - Caregiving relationships are a messy business at times, and you can't control them by putting on false cheer or helping harder. Since your Two tendency is to only see your positive motivations, you may feel shame around any part of you that you perceive to be selfish.

Indirectness - You tend to hide real desires and motivations by being less than direct with your Loved One and others. If you hide your truth or send mixed messages, others will sense it and may hold back.

Two's Opportunities for Personal Growth

You focus on the positive. You think you know what others need and tend to be free with advice and also gifts. You might not like seeing your flaws but are quite open to helping fix flaws in others. Part of your growth during this time is to identify your limitations as normal while realizing that others often accept you even better for your being human. For Twos

to grow, take these steps:

Self-knowledge - Ask yourself, What reflects your personal self ? What do you feel and want? What makes you unique? What do you stand for? What will give you the solid feeling you are loved? Are you loved for more than just for pleasing your Loved One? These questions, relating to self-discovery and development, will help to spark your creativity.

Honesty - The more honest you are with yourself and others in the family, the more others will trust you. Keep a positive focus, yes, but also open up to your own insecurity. They will find your vulnerability to be authentic and appealing. Accept yourself, and then grow in the knowledge that others can better relate to you.

Self-care - There is nothing wrong with some selfishness. You don't need to smile all of the time, working to convince others that you are the helper. Expand your ability to help yourself. Rather than constantly making connections, spend some time alone to identify and attune to personal needs.

Identify your needs. We all have needs—admit it when you feel needy. Make a list of every need and desire you can think of. Study each one and resolve to feel good about it. How can you meet that need? Ask for what you want. If you notice you have shame around any needs, allow those feelings to be and relax around them. Don't blame others, if they don't instantly give to you. Treat yourself the same way you would treat someone you care about, continually bringing your mind back to you when it focuses too much on others.

Be more receptive. Giving is not necessarily better than giving, and you don't have to give to receive. Giving and receiving happen naturally, but for others to give to you, you have to be receptive. You may at times feel embarrassed at what feels like too much attention. Relax and feel the joy and good feelings of others' appreciation and gifts.

Let go of territory. You can be quite territorial about your relationship with your Loved one—This is my person to give to and receive from. You don't have exclusive rights in the gifting area, so don't see others as a threat. Control yourself rather than others. If you control or cling too much, you might lose the very thing you want to keep, connection. If you feel this is happening, talk about it. Allow in some uncomfortable feelings.

105

Say no. You say Yes easily but can have a hard time saying no. When you feel you would like to say no, don't just imply it— say it straight up. No! Be direct. Hints and implications cause confusion. Agree to do what you can, as you can, and refuse to do more than that. Say No at least a few times a day just for practice. It won't mean that others will stop trusting or liking you.

Know that no one owes you. You may at times create unconscious contracts, thinking that others will pay up later. Be careful with these fantasies. Don't give past the point of no return. If you feel others owe you, notice how you set this up and perhaps talk about it. Give in more limited ways, so that if others don't give back, you're okay. Be aware of your conscious or unconscious expectations. Keep a journal about it.

The Two's Heart, Soul and Mind

As one of the feeling types (along with Threes and Fours) Twos live first from their heart. Their spirituality is naturally expressed from a heart place. And their thoughts are centered around relationships as that is where they live.

Twos in Relationship

Because Twos are mainly focused on getting their needs met through relationships, as caregivers you not only feel responsible for your Loved One's happiness, your own self-esteem and pride are also deeply invested. You may find yourself projecting that your Loved One needs pleasing 24/7. In normal times, the balanced Two pleases herself as well as others and it is easier on everyone. But in these trying times that balance can seem almost impossible to tend to, let alone achieve. Twos will do anything to please all of their Loved Ones. They alter themselves

to satisfy others, and nothing is too much to give if they are appreciated. The intensity and amount of a Two's giving is great in normal times. Add on the perceived requirements of this and the Two's giving becomes monumental.

Some Twos are right on target, giving only what their Loved One needs. Others give what they think is needed or even what they need themselves, giving to themselves in the guise of giving to the other. Though more developed Twos can do well with occasional feedback, most Twos feel criticized if their intention, time, and energy aren't appreciated.

Relationship Advice - As a Two you need to see that there are many ways to relate apart from giving, such as receiving from your Loved One; sharing activities; learning together; expressing difficult emotions to allow your Loved One to be the giver; or backing off to let others manage.

Notice the ways that your Loved One likes to give which may differ from yours. Then let go of your rigid ideas of love or expand them. Be open to love showing up in new and, for you, different ways.

Trust that life can work when you let go and allow others to take care of themselves. It is one way of empowering others, rather than doing for them what they could do for themselves.

Two's Spiritual Side

As a Two, it is likely that you have a positive view of life and believe that the higher forces will support you, if you give. Good things will happen to good people. It is a risk, of course, because Twos bank on their accounts earning interest if others like their giving.

Two's spirituality often is expressed through affirmations, or otherwise maintaining an uplifted spirit. Two's focus on beauty is part of their spirituality, creating beautiful environments that possibly include art with angels, Madonna and child, happy people, and blissful nature scenes. You look toward the bright side of life and help to create a life for your Loved One that is bountiful, full of life, promise and joy.

A Spiritual Lesson - Trust that the universe will work, whether you give or not. Your spirituality increases as you surrender to life, see everything as a part of the whole, and accept that your needs will be met as a natural course of events. Relinquish your pride that thinks you know what is best for your Loved One and others.

How Twos Think and Make Decisions

Since your main focus is relationships, you think about loving connection, upsets, and what to do about being misunderstood. You are constantly planning how to give, and imagining positive outcomes from your giving. You concentrate on how to affect your Loved One and others, figuring out what would work, based on what you need this journey to be.

The average Two makes decisions most easily for others. They are confident which decisions should be made, but occasionally these decisions benefit them more than their Loved One. They can mask their own gratification in their actions for others, afraid that they will seem selfish if they make choices solely for themselves. Since the helper image is important and they want to please, the diminishment of anyone's love would be devastating.

However, people may feel guilty or beholden to you if everything you do is for them. In its extreme, excessive giving can breed resentment in others. Concealing your own needs can be a burden to others who would rather you were more self-centered.

Two's inner conversations are: I can help you.

I hope I look okay.

I want her to appreciate me.

I'm feeling awful. I wish I could reach out for help. I wish I didn't have to focus so much on others.

Two's Thought/Action Alternatives

Consider consciously and openly thinking of your own needs and outcomes. Give less, ask for more, and give more to yourself. Explore your creative side, spending quality alone time. Indulge in a massage or some other treat. Try making some decisions based on intuition, rather than controlling the wellbeing of others. Share your needs with others.

What Twos wish they could say:

I can't help you, but I know someone who can.

I decided to dress casually today. I feel better that way. She is preoccupied, but I trust that she appreciates me. I'm down. Can you listen to me?

It was fun spending time. It is nice just to hang out.

Making the Most of Being a Two

Two's modifiers, Eight, Four, One and Three, do much to ground and focus the Two, keeping her from giving until she gives herself away.

Two's Stress Type - The In-Charge Eight

Growth Type – The Unique Four

Twos generally try to repress anger in an attempt to be nice and caring and good, but under stress they go to Type Eight, The In-Charge Caregiver. This dramatic shift is usually triggered by a perceived lack of appreciation. When you slip into your Stress Type Eight, you easily damage trust and relationships. You can suddenly begin telling your Loved One, your family, and the medical professional what they need to do, with no ifs, ands, or buts. If they don't follow your dictum, you may dole out the consequences. When you're in Eight, you can unload your anger, feel righteous, and tell others how they miss the mark as human beings. In key intimate relationships that are challenging, you may even find yourself bypassing sweetness to bluntly express how hard it is to be with them. To escape damaging relationships, your most constructive route is to combine your tact and giving ability with the best traits of Type Eight—being more direct and honest. Practice being that positive Two/Eight mix, and your relationships will become more clear, personal, healthy, and satisfying.

The Growth Type for Two is Four, the Unique Caregiver. The positive side of Four is a healthy dose of creativity, self-awareness, and attunement to feelings. From the Four, Two can learn to focus on her own feelings, individuality, and self-reflection, and to value the shadow side of life. Twos are other-focused, while Fours are self-reflective and often absorbed with inner feelings. Twos are by nature afraid of fear, pain, anger, and other self-centered emotions. As a Two, when you go to Four, you have a chance to accept your feelings as well as your individuality. You may find solace in a Four-ish awareness of personal nobility, honor, and even beauty in caring for someone else. You'll find you are able to spend time alone to relax, reflect, or create, to give to yourself as much as you do to others. You integrate as you open up to your Four's self- expression through art, drama, music, or poetry. Giving is balanced by individuality and self-care.

Two's Wings – The Precise One & The Achieving Three

The way a Two manifests depends somewhat on her Wing Types. A Two's self-oriented giving may be moderated by the broader giving morality of the One. And a Two's need to be liked can be mitigated by her Three wing's drive to succeed in the world.

If you have a strong One wing, you will be more service-oriented, serious, and moralistic. You will be drawn to the social work or therapeutic aspects of caregiving. You are more of a perfectionist and not as extroverted. But One's influence can have you trying too hard to be good. You may even be critical and controlling, and then seek validation for your giving and goodness. Or you may disempower your Loved One by reinforcing his/her helplessness so that you can be of help.

Twos with a strong Three wing are more success-driven. You want to perform as the top giver. For you, it may be easier to let go of whether others like you, in order to get the job done well and get the rewards. But Three- like competitive concerns about your image, if not moderated, may supersede serving the real needs of your Loved One.

Two's Degrees of Balance

Well-balanced Twos are generous and tuned in to what others need, expecting little in return. You also know how to give to yourself, are direct about your needs, and are aware of your Loved One and other family members' limitations. You delight in relating, giving, and watching your Loved One develop. In general, you trust life will be positive, no matter what the ups and downs.

Average Twos give but expect return. You still manipulate to get people to relate to you in the ways you want, but you develop by being clear about your expectations and realizing that there are many ways for people to give. Your learning is to receive graciously. You're learning that you have needs too and needn't be ashamed of them. The more honest and relaxed you are, the more you'll have that right balance of giving and receiving.

Out-of-balance Twos strongly manipulate to get appreciation. When acts of "generosity" are not what your Loved One wants, you can respond with anger at their lack of gratitude. You don't take care of yourself but expect others to be there for you. You hold on to your Loved One for dear life, forgetting to tend to your own mature autonomy and independence.

Chapter 8: Wings And Instinctual Sub

Types

Synopsis

A person's basic dominant type is often modified or highly influenced to some degree by its neighbors. This theory manifests itself as a certain 'wing'.

There is a theory that also influences the enneagram types greatly besides the wings – it is the instinctual sub-types.

Offshoots

• If you are a type 2, you may have a wing of type 1 or type 3.
• This can be summarizes as a 2 with wing 1 or a 2 with wing 3.
• If you are a type 9, you may have a wing of type 1 or type 8.
• This can be summarizes as a 9 with wing 1 or a 9 with wing 8.

A person who is strongly influenced by one side manifests only one of the wings. A person who is strongly influenced by both sides (or none at all) is considered a person with balanced wings or 'no wings' (meaning that they are a pure personality type of their dominant type without the influence of their neighbor).

No matter how strong a person's wing, it does not change the fundamental type of the dominant personality.

In other words, two people may have the following   characteristics:
• 2 with wing 3 (Helper with Achiever Wing)
• 3 with wing 2 (Achiever with Helper Wing)

They both can still be really different with one another though they may share the common dominant type and wing.

A simple way to summarize this is that you will always have a chocolate flavored ice cream but it is completely different from an ice cream flavored chocolate – meaning the CORE type never changes and so do their   primary   functions.
The subtypes are typically manifestations of a person's instinct as they deal with the world.

The instinctual energies are expressed in such a way that each person who has the dominant   type   may   manifest   their instinctual energies in different ways.

The 3 instincts are:
- The self preservation variant
- The sexual or one-to-one variant
- The social variant

Self preservation types tend to focus more on their personal safety, their well being, natural resources, their nest egg, health and are generally more reserved compared to the sexual or social variant.

Sexual types tend to focus strongly on the chemistry or the connection between one individual and another. They are not necessarily driven by sex drives but more as a way of expressing their relationships through intimacy or deep emotional connection. Unlike the social sub-type, they prefer to have a few very close friends or a strong intimate relationship.

Social types on the other hand are not that fixated on primary intimacy. They function well in groups and are leaning more towards many personal connections rather than intensity or intimacy. There a theory that when a child is born, they need to feel safe, secure and well fed.

Failure to meet this need throughout one's childhood leads to a person developing a self preservation variant which is mostly fixated on their own survival.

If a child's physical and safety needs are met but emotional connection is absent, a person might grow up to become a sexual variant as they long and seek intimacy with others which often times is absent when growing up with one or both parents.

If both needs are well met, they become healthy social types. There may be exceptions to this rule of upbringing but it is often a recurring pattern among subtypes.

Chapter 9: The Enneagram Of Personality

Enneagram is a system or inventory of interrelated personality types for understanding human behaviour and psyche. The Enneagram is a nine-pointed star drawn inside a circle and each point represents a particular personality type (also known as an enneatype). Furthermore, this unique inventory system allows us to gain an insight into how human beings behave in various situations. It enables us to appreciate and understand our personalities and those of others too.

Now let's take an in-depth look at the captivating and often disputed 4000 year history of Enneagram and how it attained its current level of prominence. The Enneagram has its roots in Greek philosophy and was coined from two words 'ennea' which means nine and 'gramma' which means 'symbol or figure.' Some scholars have linked the Enneagram of Personality to one of the teachings of Greek monk, Evagrius Ponticus, in the fourth century AD.

The book titled 'Logismoi' highlights nine evil thoughts or temptations that give rise to all human sinful behaviours. These thought patterns include love of self (which he considered the most powerful), gluttony, greed, sloth, sorrow, lust, anger, vainglory and pride. According to him, understanding these thought processes will enable the individual to identify his or her strengths and weaknesses and also overcome the temptation to engage in sinful behaviour. Another Greek philosopher who goes by the name Plotinus, in his work titled 'Enneads' discusses nine divine qualities that manifest in human nature.

The current framework on which Enneagram of Personality is based upon, developed in the 21st century and of all the people who made major contributions to the study of Enneagram in the last hundred years, the work of Oscar Ichazo has been the most significant. He identified the nine ways in which a person's ego becomes fixated within the psyche at an early stage in life and each of these ego fixations represent the core of self image upon which the individual's personality is built. According to Oscar Ichazo, each ego fixation is also supported at the emotional level by a particular passion or vice. The main psychological connections between the nine ego fixations can be shown on a diagram having nine points. This diagram of Enneagram is known as the enneagon. Oscar Ichazo believed, a person's fixation or personality type is rooted in subjective experiences from childhood and by understanding these fixations, an individual can reduce or even overcome suffering and other limitations. The teachings and writings of Oscar Ichazo were intended to assist people transcend the challenges and limitations caused by deep- rooted thinking patterns and behaviour.

The Enneagram personality model has nine personality types as shown below;

1.Reformer and perfectionist - individuals with a strong desire to be perfect

2. Helper and Giver - individuals with a strong desire to be needed or feel valuable

3.Achiever and performer - individuals with a strong desire to succeed

4.Individualist and romantic - individuals with a strong desire to feel special or loved

5. Investigator and observer - individuals with a strong desire to perceive or sense

6. Loyalist and skeptic - individuals with a strong desire to feel secure or safe

7. Enthusiast and epicure individuals with a strong desire to avoid pain

8. Challenger and protector - individuals with a strong desire to oppose people

9. Peacemaker and mediator - individuals with a strong desire to avoid conflict

Enneagram is subdivided into three main categories which may be referred to as centres or types of intelligence and they are;

- Body is the physical component and encompasses types one, eight and nine

- Head is the mental component and encompasses types five, six and seven

- Heart is the emotional component and encompasses types two, three and four

These three centres also corresponds to different types of actions as explained below :

- EMOTIONAL CENTRE involves the attribute of relating to others. The strength of types two (helper), three (achiever) and four (individualist) lies in their emotional intelligence and the ability to relate and get along with others. They easily have deep concern for and empathy towards others. They focus on meeting the demands of their relationships, work or careers, family and so on and so forth. They are also driven to succeed and stay devoted to whatever they choose to get involved in.

- MENTAL OR INTELLECTUAL CENTRE involves thinking. The strength of types five (investigator), six (loyalist) and seven (enthusiast) lies in their cognitive or mental intelligence. They have the natural ability to think clearly and deeply about things and develop ideas or solutions. They have an exceptional ability to think rationally and delve beneath the surface of ideas, issues and concepts. They focus on gathering and acting on accurate and adequate facts or information. They crave stability and safety and prefer to have a host of options to choose from.

• PHYSICAL OR INSTINCTUAL CENTRE involves the act of doing. The strength of types one (reformer), eight (challenger) and nine (peacemaker) lies in their instinctive intelligence. They have the natural ability to sense what is not obvious to other people and push through with drive and determination. Those in this category focus on being in constant control of themselves and any environment in which they find themselves. This implies that their personal security and social belonging means a lot to them. They are also known to tame action in practical ways.

A detailed analysis and explanation of these personalities will be made in the subsequent chapter.

The Enneagram has a broad range of application areas including -

● MANAGEMENT AND LEADERSHIP - Being a leader or manager requires that you get work done and achieve results through people. The Enneagram Personality technique helps you build effective teams, inspire people, communicate better and improve your working relationships.

● RELATIONSHIPS - You will improve your relationship with family, friends and associates when you get a good grasp of your Enneagram personality type. It would enhance better communication and also minimise conflict situation because your needs and expectations will be clearly communicated.

● PERSONAL DEVELOPMENT - Enneagram helps you to better understand yourself and identify your strengths, weaknesses, values, preferences and drives. When this happens, you can then work towards becoming a better you, improving your strengths, overcoming your weaknesses and limitations and making any necessary adjustments to your life.PROFESSIONAL DEVELOPMENT - By understanding your Enneagram personality will make a significant difference in your career as it would enable you to identify where your aptitude lies and which career path to take.

• SPIRITUALITY - Enneagram personality techniques have been widely used across different religions for creating self awareness, meditation and spiritual growth. This is one of the few personality typologies that fit that purpose and is of great benefit to users regardless of your faith or religious inclination.

These are just a few benefits that can be derived from the use and application of Enneagram in finding and understanding our personalities. Now, let's examine some of the characteristics and principles that has made Enneagram one of the most successful and widely used models in the world.

The Enneagram of Personality is a unique model and possesses certain principles that distinguish it from other personality inventories -

●No personality type is better or worse than the other. Each of the nine personality types are unique in its own way with positives and negatives associated with all of them

●The usage of Enneagram differs from one individual to another. For some, discovering their Enneagram type may happen within a short period of time but for others it could take a relatively longer period.

●Your Enneagram personality type is just one aspect of your being. Who you are is also determined by your gender, profession, age bracket, culture, ethnicity, race and other relevant factors

●You cannot make a switch from one Enneagram type to another and you cannot create it too. Your Enneagram personality type is discovered and not created and once that happens, it cannot be changed.

●We all manifest the characteristics of each Enneagram personality type in varying degrees. The type whose characteristics an individual exhibits the most is his or her position or place in the Enneagram of personality.

●The Enneagram typology is universal in nature and can be applied to individuals from varied cultures, age groups, ethnicities, religions, races, occupations, nationalities and gender.

As useful as the Enneagram of Personality may seem, it still has its own shortcomings and therefore cannot be regarded as faultless and an all-encompassing theory or model of personality. And this is the reason why it is better used or applied by professionals or practitioners who have been thoroughly trained in the art and science of the Enneagram. Few of the limitations of Enneagram of Personality are as follows -

•The results of using Enneagram or taking an Enneagram test can be different from an individual's expectations and this may cause the individual to either ignore or reject the results altogether. Enneagram of Personality may identify an individual as a particular personality type which he or she may not agree with

•For the outcome of an Enneagram test or analysis to be reliable, it should ideally be applied by a competent professional like a counsellor, human resource expert, management consultant or psychologist. This is because there is a huge possibility that an individual user may not apply it correctly.

•Even when it is handled by trained professionals, the results may not be scientifically valid or identify the true personality type of the individual. The Enneagram of Personality test can be affected by uncontrollable factors or conditions.

In this chapter, we have examined the following -

●An introduction to the concept and history of the Enneagram of Personality

●An overview of the nine personality types in Enneagram

●The benefits and demerits of the Enneagram of Personality

We will now examine each of the Enneagram personality types in much greater detail. In doing so, specific criteria will be used to examine each of the personality types in order for us to be able to make comparisons in the right context. In the next chapter, we will examine the peculiar nature of the Type One personality in the Enneagram model.

If you're enjoying this audiobook so far, I would appreciate it so much if you went to Audible and leave a short review.

Chapter 10: Enneagram Starting Point

"The process of transforming the heart can be difficult because as we open it, we inevitably encounter our own pain and become more aware of the pain of others. In fact, much of our personality is designed to keep us from experiencing this suffering. We close down the sensitivity of our hearts so that we can block our pain and get on with things, but we are never entirely successful in avoiding it. Often, we are aware of our suffering just enough to make ourselves and everyone around us miserable. Carl Jung's famous dictum that "neurosis is a substitute for legitimate suffering" points to this truth. But if we are not willing to experience our own hurt and grief, it can never be healed. Shutting out our real pain also renders us unable to feel joy, compassion, love, or any of the other capacities of the heart.", Don Richard Riso, The Wisdom of the Enneagram

The Enneagram Personality system is a powerful tool. It can help you understand the motivations of others but perhaps most importantly it can help you understand your own self! I could spend chapters waxing lyrical about the benefits and uses of the Enneagram but if you are like most people. At this point all you want to know is which type you are!

When you attempt to find your Enneagram type you need to concentrate on your general personality. Namely what you have resembled over an extended period of time or most of your life to date.

The greatest mistake one can make while doing this evaluation is to do it for the sake of doing it without examining yourself properly. This frequently results in marred results and unreliable findings. You have to be prepared to take the good with the bad. If you are doing this as an exercise to find out how wonderful you are then you may be in for a depressing wake up call.

In order for this test to work properly, you have to ensure you answer everything truthfully, without filtering the answers or by lying to yourself.

For example, you could be faced with a choice between assertiveness and shyness. Though one wishes to be more assertive, you have to be really truthful with yourself about where you are the majority of your life and not claim to be self-assured or desire to be more - it doesn't work if you think into the future to establish who you wish to be. You must be where you are right now - this is your true nature.

Once you figure out who you are, there are numerous online Enneagram tests that will reveal to you 3 things:

- Your dominant type

- Your wing

- Your instinctual sub-type

Record these down in addition to the 2nd and 3rd results of the test. Often times, the script will generate a set of results that is most likely your personality. Make sure to examine the results of the 2nd and 3rd probability, as it is important for you to consider all the possibilities particularly when all the results are really close to each other.

If you are a type 5 (investigator/observer) like me, it means that you are born into that type. You have been that type all your life and it doesn't change.

You may argue that a person experiences growth throughout their lives. You may object to being labeled by pointing out your considerable development over the years. While it is true you have matured and grown into a more rounded human being. This doesn't mean that your type shifts, it means that you have developed from an unhealthy type into a more healthy character type. Remember that no one Enneagram type is better or worse when compared to the others. Growth and development just mean that you are growing from one health level to another.

Each type has its onsets of strength and weaknesses that follows that individual throughout his/her life.

For every single type, there is a set of primary motivations that associate itself with that type. This can be encapsulated into the following:

- Ego Fixation

- Holy Idea

- Basic Fear

- Core Desire

- Biggest Temptation

- Greatest Vice

- Virtue

Keep in mind that every individual is totally different. Two individuals of the same dominant Enneagram type may appear and function different outwardly, but their basic core preferences in life is exactly the same.

One of the most important reasons to learn about the Enneagram of personality is to better understand yourself. Some people get a little depressed when they first get into this fascinating subject. They look at the negative tendencies of their type and assume that they are stuck with these problems and there is nothing they can do to change the reality. I have not found this to be true.

We all have a built in propensity to avoid aspects of our life that we are afraid of. We label these as things that we don't like or can't do. For example I am a type 5 and as such I have all the introverted, deep thinking tendencies that go with this particular Enneagram type. I have always declared quite openly that I have no rhythm and I can't dance to save my life. When I learned about this system I realized that this belief is just a lie I have been telling myself to avoid going near an extroverted area of life that I don't find comfortable.

What has changed in my mindset around this specific issue is I now understand why I don't like to dance. It is not that I am incapable of doing it; it's not that I couldn't learn to be a very good dancer if I put the time and effort in. The truth is I have avoided this aspect of life and given myself permission to fail because my type finds it uncomfortable.

We all have blind spots in our personalities that we avoid because we have told ourselves that we are not very good at a particular thing. Perhaps yours is that you believe you are not a good public speaker or you could never learn to swim. It doesn't matter what area of life is specific for you, I know for certain that there are things that you have pre-decided that you are no good at.

The great news is, with a little study of the Enneagram and some investment in yourself, you can quickly identify the areas of your life where you are not giving enough focus. Then you can make an informed decision as to whether your life would be better if you were stronger in this area or not. Perhaps me becoming a better dancer won't enhance my life massively. However, I am sure you can see how maybe someone becoming a better public speaker could make a dramatic difference and improvement to his or her career.

If you have studied the law of attraction you will already know that your thoughts become things. Because I believe that I am a terrible dancer I create a self-fulfilling prophecy. However, it is a little more complicated than that. The law of attraction will also give you more of what you don't want. The more you think about what you don't want or the more you feel afraid of something the more you will get of that situation and the corresponding emotions that go with it.

Someone at some point has probably challenged you to try and not think about a pink elephant or to not be aware of your right foot. It's impossible to do because of the way our brain works. In order to not think of something you have to think of it first – it's a paradox. What we can correlate from this action of our mind is that you can't push away the things about yourself you do not like. Any action much have a corresponding reaction. Life is like being inside a giant revolving door, the harder you push the door in front of you away the harder you are going to get hit in the back of the head. Ergo, the harder you try to avoid or push away the weak areas of your personality type, the more fuel and energy you feed into them.

Chapter 11: The Fractal Enneagram

This diagram, which generated considerable excitement the first time I showed it to anyone who understood these matters, presents a visual insight into one of the most essential features of the diagram, which is dynamic and works on multiple levels. Again, quotes from **In Search of the Miraculous** are used to introduce the basic concepts.

Gurdjieff explained in some detail that in the enneagram, every note forms the do for a subordinate octave beneath it.

His original remarks to Ouspensky on this matter are as follows:

In the study of the law of octaves it must be remembered that octaves in their relation to each other are divided into fundamental and subordinate. The fundamental octave can be likened to the trunk of a tree giving off branches of lateral octaves. The seven fundamental notes of the octave and the two 'intervals,' the bearers of new directions, give altogether nine links of a chain, three groups of three links each.

The fundamental octaves are connected with the secondary or subordinate octaves in a certain definite way. Out of the subordinate octaves of the first order come the subordinate octaves of the second order, and so on. The construction of octaves can be compared with the construction of a tree. From the straight basic trunk there come out boughs on all sides which divide in their turn and pass into branches, becoming smaller and smaller, and finally are covered with leaves. The same process goes on in the construction of the leaves, in the formation of the veins, the serrations, and so on."

...In order better to understand the significance of the law of octaves it is necessary to have a clear idea of another property of vibrations, namely the so-called 'inner vibrations.' This means that within vibrations other vibrations proceed, and that every octave can be re**sol**ved into a great number of inner octaves.

Each note of any octave can be regarded as an octave on another plane.

Each note of these inner octaves again contains a whole octave and so on, for some considerable way, but not ad infinitum, because there is a definite limit to the development of inner octaves.

These inner vibrations proceed simultaneously in 'media' of different density, interpenetrating one another, they are reflected in one another, give rise to one another; stop, impel, or change one another.

Let us imagine vibrations in a substance or a medium of a certain definite density. Let us suppose this substance or medium to consist of the comparatively coarse atoms of world 48, each of which is, so to speak, an agglomeration of forty-eight primordial atoms. The vibrations which proceed in this medium are divisible into octaves and the octaves are divisible into notes. Let us imagine that we have taken one octave of these vibrations for the purpose of some kind of investigation. We must realize that within the limits of this octave proceed the vibrations of a still finer substance. The substance of world 48 is saturated with substance of world 24; the vibrations in the substance of world 24 stand in a definite relation to the vibrations in the substance of world 48, namely, each note of the vibrations in the substance of world 48 contains a whole octave of vibrations in the substance of world 24. These are the inner octaves.

The substance of world 24 is, in its turn, permeated with the substance of world 12. In this substance also there are vibrations and each note of the vibrations of world 24 contains a whole octave of the vibrations of world 12. The substance of world 12 is permeated with the substance of world 6. The substance of world 6 is permeated with the substance of world 3. World 3 is permeated with the substance of world 1. Corresponding vibrations exist in each of these worlds and the order remains always the same, namely, each note of the vibrations of a coarser substance contains a whole octave of the vibrations of a finer substance.

If we begin with vibrations of world 48, we can say that one note of the vibrations in this world contains an octave or seven notes of the vibrations of the planetary world. Each note of the vibrations of the planetary world contains seven notes of the vibrations of the world of the sun. Each vibration of the world of the sun will contain seven notes of the vibrations of the starry world and so on.

The study of inner octaves, the study of their relation to outer octaves and the possible influence of the former upon the latter, constitute a very important part of the study of the world and of man. **(Ouspensky, 134-136)**

Chapter 12: Enneagram Test

Let's do a quick recap of the main personality types before you jump into our interactive online test:

Type one: Reformer

If this is your primary type, your focus is to make the world "right" based on your perceptions. You are purpose driven, set high standards for yourself and are very self-controlled.

Type Two: Helper

If this is your primary type, then you are driven by the need to give and take care of others. You're generous, empathic, humble and nurturing. There's a deep longing to feel loved and accepted and at times the giving can be done in an effort to secure that state of being loved.

Type Three: Achiever

If this is your primary type, then you're more focused on being the best. You want to be perceived as successful by others. You're usually very assertive, winning is everything and your personal image matters a lot.

Type Four: Romantic

If this is your primary type, then your more artistic in all you do and you have an impeccable eye for beauty. You're more attuned to your emotions and that of others and can sometimes be quite dramatic. You're a romantic at heart, and your inner fantasy world is a sanctuary to be treasured.

Type Five: Observer

If this is your primary type then your focus in on knowledge and gaining more wisdom. You're highly intellectual with a deep hunger for new ideas and greater understanding. You can articulate new paradigms in a visionary way and although you prefer solitude, when invited to speak on a topic you're passionate about you can be very welcoming and engaged.

Type six: Loyalist

If this is your core personality type, then you're full of courage. You are trustworthy and self-reliant. You often struggle with self-doubt and doubting others, which can create a rollercoaster of emotions for you, but when you're not in doubt, you're very committed and decisive.

Type seven: Enthusiast

If this is your primary type, then fun and spontaneity is your thing. You're fun, playful and pleasant to be around. You have a very positive outlook and savor the richness of the world. You tend to get easily distracted though, and you always seem to be moving to the next exciting adventure, but when not scattered around or distracted you have the potential for tremendous accomplishments.

Types eight: Challenger

If this is your primary type, then you are intense! You like to be direct with others. Productivity, high energy and excellence in your work matter to you. You're self-determined, generous and you have a big heart. Others generally perceive you as very powerful which can at times make you seem a little controlling and intimidating, especially when you're trying to gain control and influence over others.

Type nine: Peacemaker

Peace and harmony is your primary drive if you fall into a type nine personality. You are authentic, unpretentious, and patient, get along with everyone, love to serve others and put their needs first. At your best, you can recognize, encourage and help bring out the best in others.

Take the test now and once you've gotten your results to go back to section II to read a more in-depth description of your type then jump into section III to figure out what kind of a layered cake you have.

Chapter 13: Why Is The Enneagram Important?

Nothing has impacted modern psychology, spiritual development and human relationship dynamics like the Enneagram tool. Millions of people all over the world have had their lives transformed through the Enneagram of Personality.

Today, it is hard to see any psychologists, coaches or therapists who don't apply the Enneagram in their service to their clients. The tool has not only revolutionized the lives of many people but has made a profound impact and contribution to various service-oriented professions. It seemed like we have found a better way to analyze and understand ourselves like never before.

Apart from the Enneagram, there are other tools for understanding people. For example, we have the Myers Briggs and the Four Temperamental Types. While these personality assessment tools are good and offer great help to know and understand people, one of the areas where they lack is finding the motivations of people.

Unconscious Motivations

The Myers Briggs will tell you how you do things, but it never tells why you do things. And you see, it does not just about knowing how you do things, you want to know what drives, compels, and propels you to take a particular action. The fact is that every action we take has an underlying motive or intention backing it. And until you know what drives you, you can't understand yourself in a deeper way.

In his book, Seven Spiritual Laws of Success, Deepak Chopra said, "Attention energizes and intention transforms. Whatever you put your attention on will grow stronger in your life. Whatever you take your attention away from will wither, disintegrate and disappear. The Intention, on the other hand, triggers the transformation of energy and information.

The Intention is the real power behind desire. It is actually desired without attachment to the outcome."

It is not what you do that matters, but it matters why you do them. Once you understand the intentions and motivations behind your actions, you can decide to focus your attention on areas that you want to experience growth in your life. As you focus your attention on the right intentions, you will see your life getting better and better.

Not only does the Enneagram personality help us to know what drives and motivates our actions, but it also helps to know the hidden dynamics of our inner life. If you could recall, one of the reasons Ichazo developed the Enneagram of Personality, was to help the people of his days to do the "inner work." If you want to change your outer life, you have to work on your inner life. How do you do that?

Centers of Intelligence

The Enneagram of Personality tells us that we have centers of intelligence in each of

154

us: thinking (head), feeling (heart), and acting/instinct (body). To each one of us, there is a pattern of thinking, feeling and behaving that is ingrained in our subconscious mind. We might not be aware of this pattern of life, but that is what we follow each and every day.

Based on your personality type, you can begin to understand your inner pattern of life. How you do think, feel and react to the world and things around you? How you do think, feel and react when things happen to you? Basically, your attitude is a reflection of your personality and your personality is a reflection of who you are. The key to changing your life is to change the way you think, feel and behave.

One of the areas of concern in the world is self-improvement. Many people have seen the need to develop and grow. But the problem is that they use the wrong solutions and systems to transform their lives. Your life is an expression of your thought life. When you change who you are inside, you will see a different person outside. This is very important!

Deadly Sins

We understand that we humans are liable to sin. We have a sinful nature that easily sways us to sin. While we can all fall prey to all kinds of temptation and commit every type of sin, you'll notice that some people are easily tempted to a particular sin to that of others. Why is that so? Well, it is due to the weakness in their personality type.

In the Enneagram, we have been told that each personality type has an associated vice or deadly sin which, at stress moments of life, shows up. All of us have the downside of life when we begin to manifest the weakness of our personality. You might appear, strong and able, but when your time of stress comes, you might fall prey to "your deadly sin."

Just take a look at the Enneagram again. This time around, you want to focus on the deadly sins of each enneatype. Check each type and the deadly sins associated with that personality. Notice, that the deadly sins are hidden in our souls—the emotions. They are what make us human. We were born with that. We all have all the deadly sins in us, but some people are just prone to some sins than others—because of the weakness of their personality type.

Figure 3: Deadly Sins/Vices of Each Enneatype

Now, when you look at the Enneagram, you'd notice that;

Type Ones (The Perfectionist/Reformer) are prone to the deadly sin of anger/wrath/serenity. They are quickly irritated by the imperfect work of other people. They want everything to be perfect, and therefore, get angry at when things are not right. They can also develop self-righteous anger when they tend to be highly religious and spiritual.

Type Twos are the Helpers. They have a need to love and to be loved. To express their motivations, they give freely and generously. Moreover, they are easy and quick to get proud of their good deeds. They feel shy to ask for help when they need it, but they are quick to offer help to others. You know the people who do well to you and then brag about what they have done to you. Their need for approval makes them do what they do to impress other people and inflate their self-worth.

Type Threes are the type highly motivated by the need to be successful. Therefore, they tend to create a good image or value to create success. They pressurize themselves to be successful. Why they do this, their personality type exposes them to the deceit which sways them from being themselves. Instead of being realistic with themselves, these people sometimes lie to themselves and other people in order to influence decisions to succeed.

Type Fours have a strong need to be unique and different. They have a deep longing for the ideal which makes them engage in the act of thinking of something special and unimaginable. They sometimes leave in a fantasy world, forgetting that what they are thinking about has no touch with reality. They are prone to envy when they look at other people's stuff and accomplishments. This tends to be discontent with what they have and long to get what other people have.

Type Fives are the investigators/researchers and thinkers. These people have a strong need to understand and acquire knowledge. Their personality type seems to make them prone to avarice. They have this negative tendency to keep on gathering and sharing little and little. Many of these types are prone to being greedy for material gain and holding on too much. Their fear of depleting drives them to hold back and avoid sharing/giving away. They seem to be the opposite of the Type 2/Givers.

Type Six are the loyal skeptics. They are prone to worry about the way other people will behave in the future. They seem not to easily trust people because they are skeptical and highly cautious of other people. When they work as security officers, they tend to flourish because they are cautious of people and make sure all assets are kept well. Yet, some of them go to the extreme.

Type Sevens are the enthusiasts. They can't help to control themselves. They want more and more, and not satisfied with what they have. They are craving more and wanting more because of their fear of deprivation. This is why their major deadly sin is fear.

Type Eights are the challengers. They can be very bossy and hard on others because of their undying quest to keep on trying new things. They tend to be uncaring and driven to lust because of their quest to get things done without caring about the concerns of other people. They start many things but they get easily distracted and never-ending what they have started.

Type Nines are the peacemakers. They have a tendency to coil in their shells when they are stressed up. You might think they are lazy and slothful, but that is how they behave in their stressful moments. They need to make peace with others tend to make them neglectful and careless about certain things.

What are your deadly sins? Which vices are you easily prone to? What are your blind spots? Once you identify your basic personality type you also want to look at the deadly sins associated with it. If you focus on improving and growing yourself, the deadly sins will be masked through your new behavior and habit patterns. The new pattern and way of life will help you to improve your personality and become a better person.

Emotional Intelligence (EQ)

In 1995, Daniel Goleman wrote an award-winning book on emotional intelligence: "Emotional Intelligence: Why it can matter more than IQ. Most people thought that when you do well at school, then you will also do well in life. Yet, Daniel Goleman's book disproved this erroneous belief in the educational circles.

Goleman said, "If your emotional abilities aren't in hand, if you don't have self-awareness, if you are not able to manage your distressing emotions, if you can't have empathy and have effective relationships, then no matter how smart you are, you are not going to get very far." You see, emotional intelligence starts with self-awareness and that is what the Enneagram tool offers. Until you are self-aware, you can't manage yourself.

There are five main components of emotional intelligence: self-awareness, self-control, self-motivation, empathy, and people skills. You have the famous ancient quote, "Know thyself." If you don't know yourself, you can't improve yourself and if you can't improve yourself then you can't get better in your life.

This is why self-awareness is very important. You can't get ahead in your spiritual, social, financial, relationship and career life if you don't get to know yourself better.

The Enneagram is like a self-revealing tool that seems to pierce into your thoughts and intentions. It reveals to you who you really are and why you do things you do. You get to know yourself better. And the other part is that the more you read and study the enneatype, the more self-aware you become and then begin to catch yourself when you behave in ways that are not right.

Once you are self-aware, you'll notice that self-control will follow. Highly disciplined people are first and foremost self-aware. They have high self-esteem and self-worth because they know who they are. The knowledge about your personality type enables you to be in a better position of controlling your emotions and behaving in a better way.

Brain Tracy said, "Motivation requires motive." If you're going to motivate yourself to achieve greater things in life, then you need to know and understand the motives that drive your actions. When you are self-aware, you tend to use your motivations to push yourself to go the extra mile. You will also eradicate motivations that will not enable you to behave right. The Enneagram tool helps us find our hidden motivates and then readjust and re-strategize.

Empathy is very important because life is made of relationships. People say that life is not fair because it is not about what you know but whom you know. Well, it is not enough to know people. You have to empathize and relate with people. And the type of Enneagram you have plays a big role in the way you act, behave and deal with other people. When you know your enneatype, it helps you to understand other people's emotions or feelings and react to them in a better way.

People's skill is the key in life. Some people are more social than others. These people are often rated as having high interpersonal skills. To do well in life, you need to have good people skills. Usually, type nines are good with people. They are peacemakers and long to avoid having issues with people. They are peaceful and try to forgo certain things just to have peace with others. They hate quarrelling and stepping on other people's toes. They have high social and people skills which make to do well with handling and managing people.

Chapter 14: Enneagram Super Heroes

You recognize that the Enneagram contains the higher attributes and fear-reactive features of nine basic types of personalities. Each of us has the higher and reactive characteristics of all nine forms, but some of them are more important to you.

Our reactive self is inflexible, pliable, argumentative, cunning, stubborn, distracting, defensive, moody, and futile. Sometimes it is difficult to notice when we react to these negative features, especially when your heart is in the right place. One good way to see this is only to note when you feel uncomfortable or somehow threatened.

superheroes are often portrayed as faulty, but good people are like us trying to make the most of their situation. To help you to visualize better the defects which sometimes mask you, our Enneagram

Super Heroes and their superego behavior are here.

Type ONE: ONEder Woman–This incredible model of perfection always knows what every situation is right. She is incredibly capable of being flawless, making no mistakes, and of wanting those around her to follow her standards.

Yikes! Yikes! Standards are relevant, but mistakes are made by people. If you always have to do things your way, even if you feel that your way is the best, allow for the possibility of many different ways of performing a task.

Form TWO: St Benevolence-This benevolent lady of goodness always gives and gives and guarantees that everyone knows how much! She never misses a chance to be rewarded for her good deeds.

Real hospitality is a reward for itself and needs no praise or acknowledgment. If you need people to know your good deeds, perhaps besides kindness, you have another motivation.

Form THREE: Captain Unbelievable — This superhero never misses a chance to celebrate his successes or his possessions. His walls are lined with his pictures of important people, and he always drops his name.

Excellence is your dedication and your work. If the praise and recognition are more important than the work itself, consider why impressing others is so important.

Form FOUR: The Dark Star–This superhero will struggle through to the end even against impossible odds while being deeply misunderstood and sadly underestimated.

The higher self does not fight and must not be known. If you feel like a victim in any part of your life, consider why you have invested so much of your self-worth with other people's approval.

Form FIVE: Cerebrain–This superhero knows everything about that thing in the world amazingly well. Celebration knows everything but little understands.

You don't have to impress anyone with your understanding if you trust who you are and what you know. When you demonstrate how intelligent you are, perhaps it is time to consider why you are so unsure.

Form SIX: Anti-Hero-This superhero has the capacity to see everyone's questionable motivations-criminal or the average person. Nobody can be trusted, so Anti-Hero waits for the action to bring it together.

It may be relaxing for about a minute to wait for stuff to break down, so you can say, "I knew it!" But watching and waiting for the worst is almost sure to make it happen. Your true nature knows that good and bad are part of every life. This acknowledges the moments when things are good and the times when things are wrong.

Form SEVEN: Adventure Man-During a thrilling moment in time, Adventure Man never really gets around fighting crime or rescuing damsels in distress. That would slow him down and take too much time. No one is quicker than this ennea-hero in the name of multi-tasking to avoid responsibility and avoid accountability.

Running your life with the speed of light is a way of avoiding your emotions and the confusion that you create in others ' lives. Your true nature doesn't rush to do anything because it knows that it has all it wants.

Form EIGHT: Commander-Doubted with the ability to maintain peace and protect the innocent, the Commander keeps tabs on every aspect of his life. Nothing leaving the chance he always offers his services to keep an eye on the world while God catches the nap.

The authentic self knows only our thoughts and responses, which we command. It's a waste of time trying to regulate everything and everyone else.

Type NINE: Amazing Disappearing Woman—This great hero is able to become invisible and to disappear into his own world whenever things become too intense. The amazing disappearing woman just pretends they don't exist when the arch villagers show their evil presence.

Your authentic self does not have to avoid problems because it knows that you have internal resources to handle whatever happens. Hiding problems makes them more challenging.

What Does the Study of Personality Do For You?

Personality is a story-like word: it's clear and familiar until you're trying precisely to define what you mean. There are so many different elements and perspectives that we find ourselves quickly in a labyrinth of generalization. They say that when people have a distinctive personality style, and we also talk about personality types, we mean that there are specific and definable ways of having a personality. It is easy to decide that it is impossible that a term so hard to describe offers us practical advice.

In reality, the contrary is true. Type of personality is a term that has emerged primarily because it has practical uses. The question probably isn't whether a human being can be represented with accuracy by any type of personality or style theory. Rather, it is worth asking why a good personality system is a useful tool to make choices to connect with any individual person. Like stories, good personality descriptions are not true or false by themselves. We explain how we understand the truth.

The first thing a good personality system does is to remind us that others don't necessarily think or respond in the same way we do. That's pretty basic and always helpful. Our natural inclination is to try a common ground when we want to interact or influence others. Like us, we often assume that the motivations, beliefs, and emotions lead to this common ground. The principle of personality encourages us to note that we can all take very different routes in the same direction. Just because we have certain things in common does not mean that we have the same ideas, values, or priorities.

The second thing that is beneficial is that a good system of character types decreases the difficulty of dealing with people. If we had to have a fair and accurate view of everyone we associate with, we would have to limit our interactions severely. In a world in which everyone is the product of a unique combination of DNA and experience, there is only too much information. Personality theories allow us to generalize and simplify so that we can devise faster. It's the best guess, not the facts, but it's more exact than everybody thinks exactly like us. Think of personality types as working hypotheses, so you can quickly figure out where to go next in an interaction or relationship.

There are many more good reasons, including a healthy curiosity about men, for researching personality theory. One thing that is worth considering is that knowing the variety of personality types will take some of the stress off your tougher ties. When you understand motivation and behavior patterns, you will see the challenges different in relationships. Paradoxically, you will take these problems less seriously by knowing personality. You will see your relations from a new angle, one that lets you be curious about how misunderstandings take place rather than how they rage.

Therapists, coaches, and authors have also researched personality theories since they can contribute to concrete methods to change the results they produce in their work. The truth is that everyone can benefit from a better understanding of how people maintain consistency in their beliefs and attitudes in a changing world. Theories about personality make it easier for us to see trends in the apparently random or inconsistent information about people around us. They enable us to understand better what we can say or do to interact more effectively.

Our comprehension of why we research personality also gives us parameters to test different theories and structures. We do not have to judge that a program is valid to support. We must find it sufficiently systematic to learn how to recognize different types and how to be practical enough to achieve good results in the application. Every credible program is a starting point. If you compare programs, you should look for one that represents the number of people you communicate with and the degree of control that you need in these interactions.

The Enneagram is a model of personality types which has evolved over many centuries and can be used and used in various degrees without paper examination. You may find it to be the right place to satisfy your curiosity and work better with others.

The Master Tool of Transformation with Enneagram

The Enneagram is an ancient device of uncertain origin, which some real geniuses claim was brought into it. The Sufi numbers are also referred to as the chessboard game and some other wonderful development stuff that has always been around.

The Enneagram reveals the strengths and disadvantages of all smart beings raised on this planet. This shows the nine basic personality styles.

This is the description of the nine forms of personalities with a modern interpretation.

1. The perfectionist, number one individual with a great deal of discipline, wants the best performance at any cost. In the films, they make pretty good villains because they don't care about human suffering; they're the ultimate inquisitor.

2. The agent or the priest, also known as the supporter. Typically they are very service-oriented, supporting others. Often they are manipulative manipulators who want us to do what they want because the only way they think is right and right in the world. A theme is a beggar who cries out.

3. The chameleon often referred to as the climber. This man is lovely and all good, but his loveliness is evident. You can see them shift before your eyes and transform as a crisis arises. Normally nobody can

believe they're fake characters because they build a nice smile and a good character outlook, while in fact, they divorce themselves from their true feelings.

4. The extra sensitive is a personality-like performer. This leads to envy and depression that other people have done with their lives. Many suicidal tendencies are likely because he understands his own urges, and he feels guilty about them at the same time. For others, it may seem that such a person exaggerates other people's emotional concerns.

5. The nerd is paranoid. This guy is very smart, but he gets distracted at the same time. In everything, he sees logical connections. He just wants to know the correct explanation for the phenomenon happening everywhere. He may become paranoid and conspiracy theories and cure-all solutions. He likes to understand his brilliant mind, and he wants to find a way to fit in with the term he feels is somehow awful.

6. The devils protect it. He could be a faithful follower or a bad sedative enemy gossiper. He has a lot of tension inside that he alleviates by finding the best possible interpretation of other people's behavior and telling everybody what his twisted mind thinks. She believes that everyone else is the worst, except the one he's loyal to. He may look like an unconcerned prick, but he's a very hard-working and masochistic guy.

7. The psychopath. The maniac. He's a peter pan, and he never grows up. He's always an unsuccessful boy. He screams and struggles for things and stuff that he wants so badly that it is even frightful. It might be food, video games, a theater ticket, you name it. He is greedy and doesn't give too often to distribute the products equally.

8. The dictator of the tyrant. He could make a big boss or dictator, too. He has a strong personality that is always grounded in the end. He may act like a mafia leader when unbalanced, threatening everyone

who does not suit his wants. He could be a true hero and philanthropist on the positive side.

9. The nine is the world's most unavailable person. A kind of peace-builder disconnected unconscious person living in a perpetual silent disconnection. He or she may go to a party with you and then forget that you're there. Sometimes, they have awakenings like that, oh my, but all this time, you were here!

In practice, the Enneagram has been used by trainers in group dynamics to construct transformation exercises that impact every part of the pool of human shadow weaknesses with the goal of overcoming it. It created the biggest breakthroughs in shadow master transformations and was a matter of very serious studies.

Chapter 15: The Reformer Subtypes

The three subtypes associated with the reformer are worry, zeal, and non-adaptable. You can learn more about these subtypes and what they mean below.

Self-Preservation: Worry

Because of their nature, reformers have a tendency to experience a high amount of worry in their lives. They are often known as perfectionists. They want everything to be under control and completed or managed in a specific way. Therefore, they use worry as a means to anticipate problems or anything that may reduce control or take away things from happening.

It is not uncommon for a reformer to be anxious and excessively prepared for nearly everything in their lives. They have a strong inner critic, with a tendency to be extremely hard on themselves. Many times, they will try to live up to unreasonable standards, and this furthers their worry because they feel they are incapable of achieving these standards.

Although the reformer often avoids expressing angry emotions, they do have a tendency to feel deep levels of frustration when they are disrupted or when things are not up to their standards. This can result in them bottling up a large amount of anger and feeling burdened by their emotions and their perceived failures or the perceived failure of others.

One-on-One: Zeal

Reformers have a very idealistic view on how things should be. They like to try and enroll others in their idealistic view, but rarely want to enroll in the ideas of anyone else. This results in them coming off as intense, and they tend to have a large impact on others. This impact can be positive or negative, depending on who the other person is and how they feel about the idealistic view of the reformer.

When they feel that their efforts are not being improved or resisted by others, the reformer will often become angry and frustrated. This can result in even more bottled up emotions. Alternatively, it can result in conflict and the reformer blaming others for their inability to experience an idealistic reality.

Social: Non-Adaptable

The reformer is known to be non-adaptable. Due to their nature, they believe that their worry combined with their meticulous attention to detail would mean that they are always right. When they are out of balance, they believe that everyone else must be wrong and will often start passing the blame to others when things are not achieved. They have a tendency to reject anyone else's views or beliefs, even those of another reformer.

The reformer typically enjoys drawing attention to what is considered to be good, right, or appropriate. They value integrity and high standards. They are known for a high level of self-control and discipline, and they find themselves both expecting everyone else to live up to their standards, while also wanting to be better than everyone else.

When they are aligned and operating at their best, reformers are rarely bothered by peer pressure and tend to be great role models. They are known to live deep in truth with their beliefs and values. Therefore, they are great at modeling how you can live your best life in alignment with your true self.

Conclusion

The Enneagram is a great tool to help you find your passion and purpose in life.

It helps you liberate yourself from all the walls you have put up to keep you safe. When your walls come down, you become open to your true self. When you are grounded in your power through your three energy centers, you will know what you need to do.

Your passions and purpose will become self-evident whenever you need to change the focus in your life.

You have all nine Enneagram types here to review, and while your type may give you clues as to what your passions and purpose are, that doesn't necessarily mean you should limit yourself to these particular interests.

When you are healthy, the universe is open to you.

You may be surprised by what your passions and purpose turns out to be.

The Enneagram helps you be honest with yourself, so you can enter into any pursuit with an open heart, mind, and body. You will be able to tell in yourself if this is an excellent choice to make.

You will also know when it is time to make a change, so just because you are passionate about something now, that doesn't mean it will never change in the future.

Finally, the Enneagram helps you be at your best so you can be compassionate with yourself when you miss the mark. It encourages you to try again, so you can learn from what didn't go as well before. You get clues on what you need to do to get healthier.

The more you feel better about yourself, the kinder you will be to others. There is a great deal more to understand and live before you start to reap the rewards of the Enneagram. But, I can assure you, with enough time and energy and self-awareness, the Enneagram is a path toward peace and contentment stronger than anything else I've ever discovered.